TEXTUAL POWER

TEXTUAL POWER

Literary Theory and the Teaching of English

ROBERT SCHOLES

YALE UNIVERSITY PRESS
New Haven and London

Designed by Margaret E.B. Joyner
and set in Times Roman type.
Printed in the United States of America by
Vail-Ballou Press, Binghamton, N.Y.

Library of Congress Cataloging Publication Data

Scholes, Robert E.
  Textual power.

  Includes bibliographical references and index.
  1. Criticism. 2. Literature—Study and teaching (Higher)
3. American fiction—20th century—Study and teaching
(Higher) 4. Deconstruction. I. Title.
PN94.S25   1985   808'.042'071173   84–19628
ISBN 0–300–03350–8 (alk. paper)

The paper in this book meets the guidelines for permanence
and durability of the Committee on Production Guidelines
for Book Longevity of the Council on Library Resources.

10   9   8   7   6   5   4   3   2   1

This book is dedicated to
five Italian girls, orphaned in Brooklyn,
who raised themselves with the help of their Church.
Four of them were serious and became school teachers.
The fifth, Carmela Maria Imello,
was frivolous, changed her name, and became my mother.
When the cosmic television camera smiles on me,
I'll wave and say,
"Hi, Mom!"

CONTENTS

PRETEXT

"A holy pretext."
"Nothing pretextual is holy."

Umberto Eco
The Name of the Rose

This book is the third in a sequence of works that I have devoted to the understanding of recent literary theory. Following *Structuralism in Literature* and *Semiotics and Interpretation*, the present study brings into the foreground a dimension of the earlier books that was less obvious in them, though some readers and critics commented on it. What they noticed in those books was a concern for the impact of theory on teaching. Their comments made me aware of another dimension of this relationship: the extent to which my whole view of theory was in fact grounded upon teaching. I see clearly, now, not only certain ways in which theory can help us solve curricular and pedagogical problems; I see also how teaching can help theory pose and articulate those problems. I see that teaching and theory are always implicated in one another. This book was written to articulate that view.

A dialogue between teaching and theory flows through this book, sometimes bringing teaching to the fore and sometimes theory. This ebb and flow of discussion and debate is unified by notions of textuality and textual power. The whole book makes an argument, more explicit at some moments than others, for shifting our concerns as English teachers from a curriculum oriented to a literary canon toward a curriculum in textual studies. This argument begins in chapter 1, with a reading of the English paradigm or "apparatus" as if it were a text. The next three chapters develop the notion of "textual power" in terms of basic classroom instruction, using very short narratives by Ernest Hemingway as illustrative texts. The following three chapters reverse the perspective, putting theory in the foreground by pursuing the major questions left unconsidered while teaching was the principal focus of discussion. The debate between "secular" and "hermetic" theoreticians over the nature of textuality is taken up in chapter 5, through discussions of works by Edward Said, Terry Eagleton, Paul de Man, and Fredric Jameson. This debate is continued in chapter 6, in a critique of the "hermetic" theory of "deconstruction" and a defense of the referential dimension of language. In chapter 7 the "secular" side of "deconstruction" is presented, through a consideration of the relationship between language and the alien in a passage from *Of Grammatology* and a motif from Ursula K. Le Guin's novel *The Left Hand of Darkness*. Chapter 8 brings us back to the classroom, with a critique of what has been a dominant approach to the teaching of composition, an approach based upon an analogy with the biological instruction of Louis Agassiz, as popularized in Ezra Pound's *ABC of Reading*. The last chapter is a defense of textual power against the ingenious assault upon it made recently by Stanley Fish.

Obviously, a book like this is an act of faith: faith that teaching can be improved or adjusted to new circumstances, that critical dialogue can refine thought, and, more specifically, that literary theory and classroom practice really do have something to say to one another. I know that many teachers feel the concerns of theory are beyond them, or irrelevant to their problems. They see theory as having kicked itself upstairs to a position where it can do neither good nor harm. While admitting that some theoreticians have earned this attitude, I would argue that practice is never natural or neutral; there is always a theory in place, so that the first job of any teacher of criticism is to bring the assumptions that are in place out in the open for scrutiny. Post-structuralist theory offers us an extremely sophisticated and powerful set of procedures for accomplishing precisely this task. That is why it is important.

On the other hand, those studies we call humanities are connected to the world that supports and nourishes them through academic institutions. Socrates did not simply want knowledge for himself, he wanted it for others as well, which is to say that he was a teacher: his dialectic was a path toward collective knowledge, gained by critical interchange. Literary theory does not exist in some pure realm of thought but in a world of institutional structures and political forces, which means that theoreticians must theorize not only over texts themselves but over the role of literary and linguistic study in the development of citizens who will themselves play many institutional roles in their lives, either critically aware or as insensitive dupes and victims. Implicit throughout this book, and explicit at many points, is the notion that reading and writing are important because we read and write our world as well as our texts, and are read and written by them in turn. Texts are places where power and weakness become visible and discussable, where learning and ignorance manifest themselves, where the structures that enable and constrain our thoughts and actions become palpable. This is why the humble subject "English" is so important and why this book is called *Textual Power*.

Though weaknesses must be visible in this text, too, I have been saved from such displays on many occasions by the timely critical assistance of friends and colleagues. Most important in this respect were my collaborator in many ventures, Nancy R. Comley of Queens College, whose observations helped immeasurably with those chapters in which teaching takes the foreground, and my colleague of many years, Michael Silverman, whose grasp of theory and willingness to share ideas have been a constant educational presence during all that time, and whose critical reading of several chapters saved me from myself on many occasions. Detailed readings and critiques of the whole

manuscript by Gregory Ulmer, Khachig Tölölyan, and Richard
Pearce were immensely useful, and discussions of particular
chapters by W. J. T. Mitchell, Michael Ryan, and Ellen Rooney
led to significant improvements in the final text. Others who
have read or heard parts of this book and responded with advice or encouragement are Jo Ann Scholes, Elaine Showalter,
Susan Gubar, Gerald Graff, Joan Scott, Geoffrey Russom,
Günter Zöller, Marlena Corcoran, Stephen Foley, Antonio
Feijo, Robert Sullivan, and Les Perlman. My thanks to all.

Some parts of this book have appeared previously: a few
pages of chapter 1—pages written in collaboration with N. R.
Comley—in Winifred Horner's *Literature and Composition*
(University of Chicago Press, 1983); a few lines of chapter 6 in
Critical Inquiry; a version of chapter 8 in *College English*; much
of chapter 9 and part of chapter 5 in *Novel*; and a version of
chapter 7 in a special printing of the Fall 1983 Mellon Lecture by
Tulane University. For permission to reprint I am grateful to the
editors of the presses and journals mentioned. The book was
completed thanks to a sabbatic leave from Brown University.

TEXTUAL POWER

1

THE ENGLISH APPARATUS

> By imagining that they have got hold of
> an apparatus which has in fact got hold of
> them they are supporting an apparatus
> which is out of their control, which is no
> longer (as they believe) a means of fur-
> thering output but has become an obsta-
> cle to output and specifically to their own
> output as soon as it follows a new and
> original course which the apparatus finds
> awkward or opposed to its own aims.
>
> Bertolt Brecht,
> *Brecht on Theatre*

> We must also describe the institutional
> *sites* from which the doctor makes his
> discourse. . . .
>
> Michel Foucault,
> *The Archaeology of Knowledge*

As individual speech acts are to the language in which they are
spoken, so are many other individual actions to the codes of the
cultures in which they occur. This is the most fundamental and
durable insight of structuralism, the insight upon which all later
semiotic studies have been founded. Every meaningful action—
wearing a necktie, embracing a friend, cooking a meal—is meaningful only to the extent that it is a sign in some interpretive code.
Human beings are aware of this and often resent it. Various
kinds of joking and wit have been developed precisely to challenge orthodoxy, to trouble the codes, to force the orthodox out
of their codified grooves of thought. Orthodoxy replies by codi-

fying unorthodox behavior, setting aside times and places for approved Saturnalias, designating certain attire as the jester's special clothing, and telling poets they have a "license" to be odd. This dialectic between codification and play is an enduring feature of human existence.

In literary or textual studies the great structuralist insight takes the form of noting that a text is to its genre as the speech act is to its language. The genre is a network of codes that can be inferred from a set of related texts. A genre is as real as a language and exerts similar pressures through its network of codes, meeting similar instances of stolid conformity and playful challenge. No one who has ever studied seriously the history of any art can doubt the importance of precedent, schema, presupposition, convention—all those things that in literary study we call genre and style—in the actual production of texts. The more one knows about a given historical situation the more one realizes the struggle behind even the smallest innovations in any art or craft, a struggle first to master and then to transcend a given generic or stylistic practice.

These two terms—*genre* and *style*—are often loosely used, and perhaps they are not susceptible to any complete clarification, but for our purposes it will be useful to make at least a rudimentary distinction between them. *Genre* refers to things regularly done and *style* to a regular *way* of doing things. In painting, landscape is a genre and impressionism is a style. Genres are social and durable; they persist through changes of style. A style is more local, often personal, as when we speak of Shakespearean comedy as opposed to Jonsonian comedy or Monet's impressionism as opposed to Renoir's. Both genres and styles, however, manifest themselves in recurrent patterns or codes that can be constructed by analyzing a set of individual texts.

Certain post-structuralists—Michel Foucault in particular— have begun studying the ways in which institutions are comparable to genres. Using this kind of approach one may consider "the prison" or "the hospital" as a generic institution, arising at a particular time and moving through history like any other systemic network of possibilities. Individual prisons may thus be seen as texts enabled and constrained by the generic possibilities of penology at a given time, just as a given literary text may be seen as an utterance based on the historically available possibilities of a literary genre. Concepts like genre and style are useful because they give us access to the invisible forces that shape textual production, just as the concept of "language" gives us access to the forces that shape our speech. In all these cases we have a material thing: this utterance, this particular text, that particular hospital or prison, seen in relation to an immaterial thing: the English language, the picaresque novel, the institutions of penology or medicine. These notions of institution, genre, and language—immaterial things with material and behavioral effects—are powerful tools of thought, whose interrelatedness has only recently become apparent. This new perception of the ways in which languages, genres, and institutions are related is leading many scholars to reconsider the dimensions of their academic disciplines, as they rediscover the very objects of their study. Anthropological analysis, as Clifford Geertz has shown in *The Interpretation of Cultures*, has come to resemble literary criticism,[1] and literary criticism now leads back toward the cultural and institutional coding of human behavior. This is happening, whether we want it to or not. The question is how we should adjust to it—"we" being members of an academic institution which is itself the invisible source of the power that controls as it enables our professional lives.

Using the strategies that have been developed in recent literary theory, I propose that we consider "English" as a generic concept, an epistemic institution or apparatus that limits and enables the specific manifestations of "English" as a discipline or field of study, including its political embodiment in this or that English department, each of which can be seen as a political and economic instance of a generic arche-department. I am not proposing a full-scale social or historical study here, but I think readers familiar with English departments will *recognize* a certain descriptive truth in the following sketch of crucial aspects of the arche-department of English that presently authorizes our professional behavior.

To sketch this invisible apparatus (as Brecht would call it) we can proceed in what is now a classic structuralist/deconstructive mode of analysis. First we will locate the binary oppositions which organize the flow of value and power in our institution; then we will proceed to criticize or undo the invidious structure of those oppositions. Though there is much in structuralism and even more in deconstruction that I find misleading or unfruitful, this combined strategy of interpretation through the laying bare of basic oppositions followed by the deconstructive critique of those oppositions seems to me immensely rich in its critical potential. It is becoming a basic part of the critic's repertory, likely to endure even the excesses of its current vogue.

The arche-institution of English lives in each one of us as a professional unconscious, revealing itself in actions and aversions that we experience in our roles as institutional beings, often under the impression that either "reality" or "our own free will" is responsible for situations and events that can be shown to have an institutionalized character. This is by no means entirely a bad thing, any more than other personal accommodations to cultural pressures are bad things, but they may become bad when new information or new events require adaptation and adjustment.. When the political or economic course of a whole society seems dangerous or dubious, an uneasy awareness of this sends ripples of institutional self-doubt through all the professions that are, in their various ways, in complicity with that society, bringing aspects of professional life that were invisible, or seemed inevitable, into the light of critical scrutiny. Such doubts, which are strictly analogous to crises in Kuhnian scientific paradigms, open fissures that enable us to perceive the initial gestures of appropriation and marginalization which have organized the institution itself. These organizing gestures can then become the basis for our analysis and critique.

The field of English is organized by two primary gestures of differentiation, dividing and redividing the field by binary opposition. First of all, we divide the field into two categories: literature and non-literature. This is, of course, an invidious distinction, for we mark those texts labeled literature as good or important and dismiss those non-literary texts as beneath our notice. This division is traversed and supported by another, which is just as important, though somewhat less visible. We distinguish between the production and the consumption of texts, and, as might be expected in a society like ours, we privilege consumption over production, just as the larger culture privileges the consuming class over the producing class (as noted, for example, by Paula Johnson in "Writing Programs and the English Department").[2]

One further distinction and our basic structure will be complete. This is the least obvious, the most problematic, and, therefore, perhaps the most important. We distinguish between what is "real" and what is "academic" to our own disadvantage. At some level we accept the myth of the ivory tower and secretly despise our own activities as trivial unless we can link them to a "reality" outside academic life. Thus we may consume "literature," which comes from outside our classrooms, but we cannot produce literature in classes, nor can we teach its production. Instead, we teach something called "creative writing"—the production of pseudo-literary texts.

The proper consumption of literature we call "interpretation," and the teaching of this skill, like the displaying of it in academic papers, articles, and books, is our greatest glory. The production of literature is regarded as beyond us, to the point where even those writers who are hired by academies to teach creative writing are felt to dwindle into academics themselves, and we suspect that their work may only be creative writing, too. How often are the works of the faculty of the Iowa Writers Workshop studied in the classrooms of the Iowa English department?

The consumption of non-literature can be taught. It is called

"reading," and most college and university English departments
are content to hope that it has been dealt with in secondary
school—a hope that seems less and less well founded as we go
on. But actual non-literature is perceived as grounded in the
realities of existence, where it is produced in response to personal or socio-economic imperatives and therefore justifies itself
functionally. By its very usefulness, its non-literariness, it eludes
our grasp. It can be read but not interpreted, because it supposedly lacks those secret-hidden-deeper meanings so dear to our
pedagogic hearts. Nor can it be produced when cut off from the
exigencies of its real situations. What *can* be produced within the
academy is an unreal version of it, "pseudo-non-literature,"
which is indeed produced in an appalling volume. We call the
production of this stuff "composition."

The structure of English as a field can then be pictured in the
accompanying simple diagram, which operates for most of us as
a semiconscious mental construct, manifesting itself concretely
in our departmental behavior, including curriculum design,
teaching assignments, and economic rewards. Both an ideology
and a hierarchy are captured in this scheme. The greatest value is
placed upon the things in the top categories, and the least upon
the things at the bottom. In many English departments we can
find sexual and economic structures mapped upon this value
system, with higher paid, predominantly male faculty members
at the top and lower paid, predominantly female colleagues at
the bottom.

What to do?

For many teachers, the proper response to this situation is
simply inversion of the hierarchy. Since composition is in demand, let the "law" of supply and demand work until composition replaces interpretation at the top of the heap. Fortunately
or unfortunately, things don't work this way. The demand for
more composition courses operates *within* a larger economic
system that privileges literature and its interpreters. As long as
the prestige system is in place, the social and economic structures of English departments will align themselves with it. Even

PRODUCTION	TEXTS	CONSUMPTION
✕	literature	interpretation
creative writing	pseudo-literature	✕
✕	non-literature	reading
composition	pseudo-non-literature	✕

if it were a good idea, the hierarchy could not be inverted. But it is not a good idea.

The proper remedy for our troubles must begin with the deconstruction of our basic system of binary oppositions itself. The whole purpose of laying bare a structure such as this is achieved only when we can complete its verbal deconstruction by practical action. This is the very point at which most "deconstructive" critics would recoil with horror from contamination by praxis. They are only too aware that praxis requires gestures of appropriation, usurpation, marginalization. One cannot act in any collective way without becoming vulnerable to later deconstruction and ultimately to critical rejection. This knowledge leads to the widespread phenomenon of deconstructive paralysis, a permanent state of equivocation before the bridge that leads from thought and writing to consequential action. The foreknowledge of guilt leads to an abdication of responsibility. This is why deconstruction is itself a *pharmakon*, a healing medicine and a dangerous drug, depending upon the amount of it that we imbibe and what other agents we mix with it.

The literature/composition opposition must not only be deconstructed in critical writing, it must be broken down in our institutional practice as well. We can begin, however, by rethinking the mental structure of smaller binary oppositions that support the great one. From this kind of rethinking a new practice can emerge.

1. *Literature/Non-Literature*. Under pressure from structuralists and post-structuralists, this distinction has already been seriously called into question. Without developing each point, let us list some of the cogent critiques of this binary opposition. First, any fragment of any text may be brought within the body of an avowedly literary text: the most banal speech or writing may appear in a novel as an aspect of characterization or setting, to great literary effect. Second, all texts have secret-hidden-deeper meanings, and none more so than the supposedly obvious and straightforward productions of journalists, historians, and philosophers. Finally, we all know that many texts that are formally literary (i.e., look like poems, plays, or stories) are of less interest than many other texts that are cast in an explanatory, meditative, or expository form. The "great books" are not all belletristic, and if belletrism falls, then any text may be studied in an English course. And who is to say that Locke or Gibbon is less valuable than Dryden or Gray? The literature/non-literature distinction cannot survive a critique that succeeds in separating literariness from value, yet that is precisely what all the formal and structural studies of the past decades have enabled us to do.

2. *Production/Consumption*. Taken in the form in which they present themselves to us, these terms are equivalent to writing and reading. The way out of our dilemma here is first to perceive reading not simply as consumption but as a productive activity, the making of meaning, in which one is guided by the text one reads, of course, but not simply manipulated by it; and, second, to perceive writing as an activity that is also guided and sustained by prior texts. The writer is always reading and the reader is always writing. The student who reads the "world" and writes about it is also sustained by other texts while producing her interpretation of whatever things or states of affairs are being considered. Some written readings are more productive than others, or more creative, but this is *never* simply a matter of the form taken by the produced text.

3. *Real World/Academy*. This is the subtlest and most pernicious distinction, rising again and again to challenge us. Schools
have been functioning as a preparation for something that
"commences" as schooling ends, but this state of affairs is not
given to us as a part of the nature of things. We have drifted into
thinking of our lives as marked by stages that are deeply divided
from one another. This has not always been so in our tradition.
Men as well as boys walked alongside the peripatetic philosophers. There are signs, now, that these rigid chronological distinctions may be losing force. Even Yale University has finally
decided that adults may actually be educable.

It can be argued that study and work may be performed by
the same person at the same stage of life but that they are still not
the same thing; and this is true, up to a point. But one who
studies in order to publish new discoveries and receive financial
rewards for them is in the "real" world, is she not?

Or is her world real only if she seeks to minimize the effort
and maximize the profit? And what of one who studies in order
to improve her own mind? This improved mind becomes the
goal and product of the labor, and any actual texts produced are
then evidences of this other, invisible product. Is an improved
mind real? Is it marketable?

I think we must answer these last questions affirmatively.
Something real is going on inside academies, but the method of
this real production has much artifice in it. Students as a class
may be defined by their involvement in what Erving Goffman
has called "practicings":

> In our society, and probably in all others, capacity to bring off
> an activity as one wants to—ordinarily defined as the possession
> of skills—is very often developed through a kind of utilitarian
> make-believe. The purpose of this practicing is to give the
> neophyte experience in performing under conditions in which
> (it is felt) no actual engagement with the world is allowed,
> events here having been "decoupled" from their usual embed-
> ment in consequentiality. Presumably muffing or failure can

occur both economically and instructively. What one has here
are dry runs, trial sessions, run-throughs—in short, "practicings." [*Frame Analysis*, p. 59][3]

There is a difference between practice and earnest, which we
must acknowledge. We err only when we make the gesture of
erecting this difference into two "worlds," one of which is held
to be all practice, the other all earnest. The neophyte drill press
operator must practice, too, before being given real projects.
More important for our purposes, however, is the fact that all
who write, whether in an ivy-covered study or a crowded office,
are involved in a process that moves from practice to earnest,
beginning with dry runs, trial sessions, rough drafts, scratchings
out, and crumpled sheets in the wastebasket. There is, then,
something inescapably academic about all writing, whether in
school or out of it, and many a text begun in school has finished
in the world. The "real" and the "academic" deeply interpene-
trate one another.

We have been considering the system of oppositions that
organizes our activities within the grip of the English apparatus.
Certainly, seeing these oppositions as problems to be resolved,
rather than as unassailable assumptions, is a step in the direction
of a new practice. But it must be followed by other, more drastic
steps. In such situations there are always those who cry out for
the most drastic solutions: "Destroy the apparatus!" they advise
us, and they mock all attempts at more gradual amelioration as
mere tinkering with a pernicious and doomed institution. In this,
as in many other questions, I find myself looking for a middle
ground between reform and revolution. The most radical talk
often produces the least action or generates an overwhelming
reaction, thus becoming literally counterproductive. On the
other hand, situations sometimes arise within institutions that
require changes too great for any tinkering to achieve them.

In my judgment the English apparatus needs a major rebuilding, and I offer that mechanical metaphor as a way of
moving beyond the revolution/reform opposition. We cannot

replace this apparatus because we are implicated in it. We cannot shut it down because it sustains our professional lives. We must keep it running while we rebuild it extensively. This will not be easy. Our analysis up to this point has revealed a hierarchical structure in which the consumption of literature is at the top and the production of pseudo-non-literature at the bottom. Another way to map this structure would be to see the teaching of literary consumption at the center of our apparatus and all our other activities positioned around it, with composition at the outermost margin. Rebuilding this apparatus is going to mean rearranging the hierarchy: repositioning or redefining literary study, because literary study is the dominant activity in this institution; it is the focus of power that holds everything else in place. We must begin our efforts at rebuilding by asking what we mean when we proclaim ourselves teachers of literature. We must mount a critique of what we do when marching under our traditional banner with the strange device that says, "Teaching Literature." The device of course does not seem strange to those who march under it. No device does. Those who march are "insiders," as Frank Kermode would say (see *Genesis of Secrecy*, passim).[4] And they usually march happily, without questioning their situation as marchers. To step outside the line of march, to scrutinize the device and see it as strange for the first time— defamiliarized, as the formalists put it—is to become, perforce, a theoretician. This scrutiny may lead to such questions as Where is the march heading? Why? For whose benefit? And what does that device mean, anyway? In recent years more and more of our marchers have stepped outside and started asking questions. We need to consider why they have done this. Something has been troubling the march itself. Somehow the fit between our practice and the world in which we practice has grown uncomfortable. Some of us can ignore the discomfort, fix our eyes on the ground, and keep marching. Others want to hoist a new banner along with the old—one that says, "Bring back the world of our comfort." But nothing comes back as it was. That is the most fundamental lesson of history.

Stepping outside the metaphor of the march, we can begin our critique of practice by scrutinizing this sign under which we have served for so long. What does it mean to "teach literature"? It does not mean that we give lessons in how to do or make literature, for that we explicitly exempt from our claims. We may indeed teach the making of pseudo-literature, or "creative writing" in some part of our establishment, but that is emphatically not what we mean by "teaching literature." In an art department the faculty is normally divided into two categories: artists and art historians. You cannot do that with an English department. The division is there, but the terminology is not. Teachers of literature would feel diminished to be called "literary historians." And the language simply has no word for the maker of literature. We cannot call our colleague in creative writing "literators" or "literatists." When William Faulkner was a colleague at the University of Virginia, the most honorific thing we could do about his designation was simply to call him a writer. The word "creative" in his case would have been too perceivable as the insult it is.

The word "literature," then, has a much higher standing in our language and culture than the word "art." The sign of this status is that empty place in our lexicon where we might expect to find the word that is to "literature" as "artist" is to "art." The prestige of literature is so great that we have a taboo against naming the one who creates it. In our culture literature has been positioned in much the same place as scripture. We have a canon; we have exegetes who produce commentary; and, above all, we have believed that these texts contain treasures of wisdom and truth that justify the processes of canonization and exegesis. When we say we "teach literature," instead of saying we teach reading, or interpretation, or criticism, we are saying that we expound the wisdom and truth of our texts, that we are in fact priests and priestesses in the service of a secular scripture: "the best that has been thought and said"—provided that it has been said indirectly, through an aesthetic medium. We will not teach Hume or Gibbon, however powerfully they think, however elegantly they write, because they are too expository or referential for us. We will bestow the name of literature only upon those texts that displace their intention sufficiently to require exegesis. We priests do love our mysteries, and the consubstantiality of beauty and truth is one of them.

This notion of literature as a secular scripture extends roughly from Matthew Arnold to Northrop Frye in Anglo-American academic life. It is linked with the rise of the study of modern literatures to a central place in the liberal arts curriculum. And it is the dissolution of this particular consensus that has been troubling us of late. Since the nineteen-sixties we have been losing our congregations, and we are scared to death that our temples will be converted into movie theaters or video parlors and we will end our days doing intellectual janitorial or custodial work.

Is there a way to avoid this fate? There is indeed, but we shall have to theorize to find it. First, we must consider what went wrong; then, we can think about making the best compromise between our dignity and the actual needs of our constituents. What went wrong with the idea of literature as secular scripture can be described simply as the loss of faith in the universality of human nature and a corresponding loss of faith in the universal wisdom of the authors of literary texts. If human nature is always and everywhere the same, then it follows that every literary text may express aspects of that great universal truth. But if human beings are constituted differently in different cultural situations, then the varieties of literature must be seen as temporal rather than eternal. If literature is not scripture, then it cannot be outside of human time.

If the text were a vehicle for eternal truth, then the teacher's function would be to guide the student toward the correct interpretation of the text, so that the truth might stand revealed. But if the text is understood as necessarily partial, its truth value various in relation to historical changes in human situations, then this sort of interpretation—what Paul Ricoeur calls "the restoration of meaning"—will not suffice. We will need a "negative hermeneutic" as well (see Ricoeur's *Freud and Philosophy*, p. 27, and Fredric Jameson's commentary on this in *The Political Unconscious*, pp. 284–85);[5] that is, we will have to restore the judgmental dimension to criticism, not in the trivial sense (discredited by Frye and others) of ranking literary texts, but in the most serious sense of questioning the values proffered by the texts we study. If wisdom, or some less grandiose notion such as heightened awareness, is to be the end of our endeavors, we shall have to see it not as something transmitted from the text to the student but as something developed in the student by questioning the text.

This question of the relationship between criticism and interpretation is a large subject that will require much fuller consideration, but at the moment we must continue to pursue our investigation of what went wrong with the tradition of literature as secular scripture. I have been suggesting that part of what went wrong was a loss of faith in the universality of human nature, and I should like to qualify this statement before moving on. Certainly, one of the reasons that those texts we call "great" persist over long periods of time is that they induce in us reflections that can be assimilated to our own situations. We feel that Milton's devils, figures like Mammon, Belial, and Moloch, are not simply collections of words but representations of human types that one may encounter today in the halls of Congress and even in our departmental meetings. Experiencing this, we are inclined to say that Milton has an insight into universal truths; but it seems to me better to understand that Milton's power with these figures, which is achieved, after all, in the rhetoric of their discourses to the assembled demons, is a result not of some disembodied genius but of Milton's developed verbal skills plus his awareness of parliamentary debates that in fact resemble our own deliberative arguments, for good historical reasons. Where Spenser's Mammon, for instance, is a miser of a type no longer actively present in our culture, Milton's Mammon not too long ago materialized as our Secretary of the Interior.

I have been using the notion of truth in characterization as a shorthand notation for the larger concept of truth in literature. My point is finally that the strengthening of our sense of history and of cultural variety has made the notion of literary truth more of a problem, requiring a more critical response, in which what is truth-for-us may be sorted out from other textual matter. Something similar must be done with respect to authorship. Scripture itself was once held to be the work of God, who was the author and guarantor of all its meanings. Hence, interpretation was the recovery of those meanings, and criticism was heresy. Now, one may be a pious Christian and still speak of the Pentateuch not as the work of God, or of Moses, but of the Yahvist, the Elohist, and various translators and redactors. Similarly, the deepest research into the lives of authors of secular literature reveals only rifts and discontinuities of personality, enacted in behavior that is often vastly different from the wisdom we have been wont to find in their literary texts. Where the texts are ambiguous, often the lives are, too. Arriving at the character of an author is now inescapably a historical, a critical, and a fictional act.

This loss of faith in the scriptural status of literature has coincided with drastic changes in the needs of our constituents. The students who come to us now exist in the most manipulative culture human beings have ever experienced. They are bombarded with signs, with rhetoric, from their daily awakenings until their troubled sleep, especially with signs transmitted by the audio-visual media. And, for a variety of reasons, they are relatively deprived of experience in the thoughtful reading and writing of verbal texts. They are also sadly deficient in certain kinds of historical knowledge that might give them some perspective on the manipulation that they currently encounter.

What students need from us—and this is true of students in our great universities, our small colleges, and our urban and community colleges—what they need from us now is the kind of knowledge and skill that will enable them to make sense of their worlds, to determine their own interests, both individual and collective, to see through the manipulations of all sorts of texts in all sorts of media, and to express their own views in some

appropriate manner. That they need both knowledge and skill is
perhaps a matter worth pausing to consider. We have sometimes
behaved as if certain skills, such as composition and even the
close reading of poems, could be developed apart from knowledge, especially apart from historical knowledge. We are paying
the price for that error now. One does not have to be a Marxist to
endorse Fredric Jameson's battle cry, "Always historicize!" (the
first words of *The Political Unconscious*.)

At any rate, the needs of our students are clear enough, and
it should also be clear that our traditional role as exegetes of the
sacred text of literature will not answer to these needs, but
perhaps this point can stand some elaboration. In an age of
manipulation, when our students are in dire need of critical
strength to resist the continuing assaults of all the media, the
worst thing we can do is to foster in them an attitude of reverence
before texts. The reverential attitude, a legacy of romantic aestheticism, is the one most natural in literary interpretation as we
have practiced it. It is the attitude of the exegete before the
sacred text; whereas, what is needed is a judicious attitude:
scrupulous to understand, alert to probe for blind spots and
hidden agendas, and, finally, critical, questioning, skeptical.

This rickety, demanding English apparatus has important
work to do in our society, but it will do this work well only if we
can rebuild it. The essential change—the one that will enable all
the others—must be a change in the way that we define our task.
To put it as directly, and perhaps as brutally, as possible, we
must stop "teaching literature" and start "studying texts." Our
rebuilt apparatus must be devoted to textual studies, with the
consumption and production of texts thoroughly intermingled.
Our favorite works of literature need not be lost in this new
enterprise, but the exclusivity of literature as a category must be
discarded. All kinds of texts, visual as well as verbal, polemical
as well as seductive, must be taken as the occasions for further
textuality. And textual studies must be pushed beyond the discrete boundaries of the page and the book into the institutional

practices and social structures that can themselves be usefully studied as codes and texts. This is what a *re*constructed English apparatus ought to do. It is, of course, also what has been attempted in these very pages.

2

THE TEXT IN THE CLASS · I

Texts are lazy machineries that ask someone to do part of their job.

Umberto Eco,
The Role of the Reader

Literary theory and classroom practice are related as any "pure" or theoretical study is related to applications in the same field. Despite the endless protests by scientists to the effect that science has no necessary connection with technology, we know that all sciences exist in a complex dynamic with technological and economic formations. The achievements of Galileo in scientific theory cannot be separated from such technical matters as the development of the telescope and such economic matters as the financial support for discovery and invention in the Renaissance. Literary theory, too, exists in a complex dynamic with classroom practice, foundation support, textbook publication, tuition payments, teaching loads, and so on. Try to imagine the New Critical revolution in literary study without *Understanding Poetry* and countless other textbooks that both changed classroom practice and provided financial rewards for those who developed effective vehicles in which to distribute the tenor of New Critical ideas.

In our time, at least, literary theory is hardly influential upon the practice of poets, playwrights, and novelists, but it is powerfully connected to the practice of teachers of poetry, drama, and fiction. That is, few poets read theory for advice on the production of poems, but a substantial portion of the audience for theory is composed of teachers. Teachers read theory in order to "keep up"—as we say—with the field of literary study, partly in response to the pressure all fashions or modes of behavior exert in this most modish of all possible worlds; partly, perhaps, for the pleasures of concentration and controversy; but also, surely, for ideas that will enhance their performance as teachers in the field of literary studies. Recognizing this situation, I wish to face as squarely as possible the question of what the recent wave of theory can actually offer us in the way of advice about what to teach and how to teach it.

Though I am convinced that the entire English curriculum needs drastic revision, I know too well the politics of change in academic institutions to suggest that such revision can be accomplished by fiat. The majority of college students, in any case, will not be working through an elaborate English curriculum. They may go a bit beyond the basic or required courses, in some instances, but many will not even do that. Our best chances to help them learn our lessons will come in those courses now called "Freshman Comp." and "Intro. to Lit." or some variant on those hallowed titles. Having spoken about our departmental structures and assumptions in the previous chapter, in this one I propose to get down to the specifics of classroom instruction.

To avoid at least some of the banality and triviality that haunt all general advice directed at specific problems (Polonius is our model here), let me make the practical situation as concrete and familiar as possible. Let us take the fiction unit of an introductory course in literary study. For X number of weeks (probably no fewer than four, no more than six) we are going to read and discuss certain narrative texts with students who cannot be presumed to know a lot about literature or to have any special commitment to literary studies. In this situation, what texts should we teach and how should we teach them? Behind that question, of course, lurk the more properly theoretical questions of *what* we are trying to teach here and *why* we are trying to teach it. My answers to these fundamental questions can be put succinctly. The object of such study ought to be *textuality*: textual knowledge and textual skills. The traditional course that "introduces" students to poetry, fiction, and drama should take textuality as its object from beginning to end, emphasizing different aspects of this object as the different literary forms are studied. Poetry emphasizes language itself and the individual subject's relationship to language. Drama emphasizes the speech act, dialogue, looking, being looked at, listening, responding. And fiction emphasizes the reductive and representational powers of language, the power to give accounts, to tell stories, to turn the world into fiction and history, to narrate.

Each of these traditional forms embodies certain aspects of textual power: the power to select (and therefore to suppress), the power to shape and present certain aspects of human experience. And textual power is our ultimate subject. We have always known this, but in the past we have often been content to see this power vested in the single literary work, the verbal icon, and we have been all too ready to fall down and worship such golden calves so long as we could serve as their priests and priestesses. Now we must learn instead to help our students unlock textual power and turn it to their own uses. We must help our students come into their own powers of texualization. We must help them to see that every poem, play, and story is a text related to others, both verbal pre-texts and social sub-texts, and all manner of post-texts including their own responses, whether in speech, writing, or action. The response to a text is itself always a text. Our knowledge is itself only a dim text that brightens as we express it. This is why expression, the making of new texts by students, must play a major role in the kind of course we are discussing.

Reading and writing are complementary acts that remain unfinished until completed by their reciprocals. The last thing I do when I write a text is to read it, and the act that completes my response to a text I am reading is my written response to it. Moreover, my writing is unfinished until it is read by others as well, whose responses may become known to me, engendering new textualities. We have an endless web here, of growth, and change, and interaction, learning and forgetting, dialogue and dialectic. Our task as teachers is to introduce students to this web, to make it real and visible for them, insofar as we can, and to encourage them to cast their own strands of thought and text into this network so that they will feel its power and understand both how to use it and how to protect themselves from its abuses.

In discussing just how we are to accomplish this task I hope to get down to details and specifics. In order to get there, however, I shall have to set up a small amount of scaffolding, drawn from recent literary theory. If we take as our immediate focus those weeks devoted to fiction in the introductory literature course, it will help to see our pedagogical goal in terms of three related skills, which I will call *reading, interpretation*, and *criticism*. These are aspects of a textual competence that cannot be divided into separate bits, but they are sufficiently distinguishable for us to understand them ourselves, *and* for us to present them to our students, as discrete enterprises that may be practiced separately, just as certain movements in dance or sport may be practiced in themselves. Let us begin with definitions.

1. *Reading*

This is the primary activity upon which the others are based. Contrary to many of our previous assumptions (including certain New Critical attitudes) reading is at least as much a knowledge as it is a skill. The supposed skill of reading is actually based upon a knowledge of the codes that were operative in the composition of any given text and the historical situation in which it was composed.

Reading is a largely unconscious activity. We can only read a story if we have read enough other stories to understand the basic elements of narrative coding. Our first stories are told or read to us by our parents, or other parental figures, who explain the codes as they go. The ideal reader shares the author's codes and is able to process the text without confusion or delay. Such a reader constructs a whole world from a few indications, fills in gaps, makes temporal correlations, performs those essential activities that Umberto Eco has called writing "ghost chapters" and taking "inferential walks"—all without hesitation or difficulty. Any hitches in this scheme will cause a shift from reading to interpretation, and certain texts are constructed to force exactly this shift.

2. *Interpretation*

This activity depends upon the failures of reading. It is the feeling of incompleteness on the reader's part that activates the interpretive process. This incompleteness can be based upon such simple items as a word the reader cannot understand, or such subtleties as the reader's sense that a text has a concealed or non-obvious level of meaning that can only be found by an active, conscious process of interpretation.

To illustrate: we may *read* a parable for the story but we must *interpret* it for the meaning. The move from a summary of events to a discussion of the meaning or theme of a work of fiction is usually a move from reading to interpretation. We feel that interpretation is a higher skill than reading, and we value and tend to privilege texts that require and reward interpretive activity. This is, in fact, one way of defining literature, and it is one reason for preferring fictional texts to thematic texts, stories to essays.

From the point of view of interpretation, stories are better than essays because essays "say what they mean" and stories do not, leaving that job for the interpreter. There is much that can be questioned in this view, but for the moment we must be content to note its ubiquity. For our present purposes it will be more important to note that interpretation can be the result of either some excess of meaning in a text or of some deficiency of knowledge in the reader.

The reverse of this situation—some deficiency in the text or excess in the reader—would seem to lead to our third mode of textual activity: criticism. It is plain, however, that excess in the reader is often projected back onto the text and is perceived as a textual excess, requiring interpretation, not criticism. This is supported by our glorification of literary texts and the reflected light from them in which we love to bask.

3. Criticism

In its trivial sense, criticism involves a claim that a certain literary work fails to achieve the purely literary norms of its mode or genre. This is the field of "taste," a mode of critical activity that has been seriously damaged by the strictures of Northrop Frye and others, though it remains essential for journalists and book reviewers. For our purposes, a more consequential sort of criticism involves a critique of the themes developed in a given fictional text, or a critique of the codes themselves, out of which a given text has been constructed.

The most striking recent examples of this sort of critical work have come from feminists, but any group that has identified its interests as a class can mount a critical attack on a story's codes and themes from the position of its own system of values. The individual reader, unless the victim of a roman-à-clef or in the grip of an invincible paranoia, is in no position to take a critical view of a text. This is so because fiction deals with types, with representative characters, and can thus be criticized only from a position correspondingly broad.

If I am right about this (and I admit it is debatable though I am prepared to debate it), then a major function of the teacher of fiction should be to help students identify their own collectivities, their group or class interests, by means of the representation of typical figures and situations in fictional texts.

In other words, instead of subordinating their human, ethical, and political reactions to some ideal of literary value—pardoning Paul Claudel for "writing well" as modernism would have it—our students should learn finally how to criticize Paul Claudel, or anyone else, from some viewpoint beyond the merely personal—and the merely literary.

My point here is that criticism is always made on behalf of a group. Even "taste" is never a truly personal thing but a carefully inculcated norm, usually established by a powerful social class. It may be objected that my definition of criticism is extra-literary and subjects literary texts to a sort of scrutiny that is unfair, not to say vulgar, denying works their very *donnée*, of which Henry James was so solicitous. Precisely! The whole point of my argument is that we must open the way between the literary or verbal text and the social text in which we live. It is only by breaking the hermetic seal around the literary text—which is the heritage of modernism and New Critical exegesis—that we can find our proper function as teachers once again.

This subject could be debated endlessly, perhaps, but I have not the patience for it and must, in any case, proceed to describe and illustrate the kind of textual study I am advocating. I have identified three aspects of such study: *reading, interpretation*, and *criticism*. Each of these can be defined by the textual activity it engenders. In *reading* we produce *text within text*; in *interpreting* we produce *text upon text*; and in *criticizing* we produce *text against text*. As teachers of literary texts we have two major responsibilities. One is to devise ways for our students to perform these productive activities as fruitfully as possible: to produce oral and written texts themselves in all three of these modes of textualization: *within, upon*, and *against*. Our other responsibility is to assist students in perceiving the potent aura of codification that surrounds every verbal text. Our job is not to produce "readings" for our students but to give them the tools for producing their own. For me the ultimate hell at the end of all our good New Critical intentions is textualized in the image of a brilliant instructor explicating a poem before a class of stupefied students. And when I see this very icon being restored to the same position within the same ivied halls, by certain disciples of Derrida—I could weep with frustration. Our job is *not* to intimidate students with our own superior textual production; it is to show them the codes upon which all textual production depends, and to encourage their own textual practice.

It is time to get down to cases, to consider how one might actually accomplish some of the ambitious program sketched out above, in such limiting circumstances as the fiction unit of a standard introduction to literature course. "With great difficulty," is the jesting answer to this question of "how," and there is much truth in it, but limitations and difficulties are the native habitat of English departments and we must work within them. Let us begin. First, we throw away our standard anthologies, because they do not give us a large enough sample of any single writer. Then we choose perhaps three collections of short stories by writers whose work will offer good contrast of styles and values: something local, something foreign; something female, something male; something obvious, something subtle; something realistic, something fantastic; and so on. One cannot encompass the world in a triangle of writers, but contrast is a basic principle here. So is interest. There is a place for the local or regional and for the internationally famous in such a triangle. At this level, however, one should avoid works too remote in culture, that need too much annotation in order to be read at all. More often than not, in such a situation, one of my authors would be Ernest Hemingway, who is justified by fame, by accessibility, and by the uses to which his work can be put.

With Hemingway's first major collection of short fiction, the volume called *In Our Time* (published in 1925 in a version only slightly different from the current Scribner's paperback),[1] one can make a substantial beginning on teaching the reading, interpretation, and criticism of fiction, as I hope to illustrate in the following section of this discusssion. (In order to do so, I must assume that my readers are familiar with this book and can consult it at need.) The book offers a number of very short texts (the "Interchapters") and others of such modest size that they can be treated with some thoroughness in a relatively short time. These factors make it an excellent book to begin with, whatever other writers of fiction the course may include.

THE TEACHING OF READING

How should we teach the short texts collected in *In Our Time?* I would begin with one of the Interchapters, using it as a way of introducing the notions of reading, interpretation, and criticism. Interchapter VII would be a good choice.

> *While the bombardment was knocking the trench to pieces at Fossalta, he lay very flat and sweated and prayed oh jesus christ get me out of here. Dear jesus please get me out. Christ please please please christ. If you'll only keep me from getting killed I'll do anything you say. I believe in you and I'll tell every one in the world that you are the only one that matters. Please please dear jesus. The shelling moved further up the line. We went to work on the trench and in the morning the sun came up and the day was hot and muggy and cheerful and quiet. The next night back at Mestre he did not tell the girl he went upstairs with at the Villa Rossa about Jesus. And he never told anybody.*

Reading involves the knowledge of two types of codes: generic and cultural. To make sense of a story *as* a story we must know in advance what a story is. The Interchapters are not all stories, of course. Many are sketches or vignettes, but even these can be used to help students refine their concepts of story, which is a basic aim of instruction in the reading of fiction. The concept of "story" is the quintessential element in the generic code of fiction.

In teaching Interchapter VII, I would begin by asking where this text becomes a story. If we had only the first six sentences would it be a story? The first seven? And so on. How much does its "storiness" depend upon changes of scene, shifts in time and place? How much does it depend upon a continuity of character? If there were two soldiers, one in the trench and another at the Villa Rossa, would it be a story? How much does it depend on a continuity of action? How much on the repetition of words? Take the verb "to tell" in its various forms, for instance. Mark them all and then discuss what "telling" has to do with this being a story. From all this and other related questions a class could begin to develop an explicit notion of fictional coding, which is one of the major guides to reading this kind of text. But to read we must also know cultural codes.

Cultural codes enable us to process verbal material: to construct a fictional "world," to orient ourselves in it, to locate and understand the characters, their situations, and their actions. Language itself is the basis of all cultural coding. One of the reasons for selecting a single, coherent book like *In Our Time* is the great advantage to be gained by the simple matter of cultural continuity that links all the stories. The more culturally at home in a text our students become, the less dependent they will be on guidance from the instructor. I hate to say it, but I must observe that one of the reasons we teachers favor the big anthology is that it keeps our students dependent upon us, justifying our existence. We must get beyond this. There are better ways to make ourselves seem useful. One of them is to *be* useful.

In teaching the cultural coding of Interchapter VII, I would begin by asking students to make explicit the ways that they construct a scene, a world, from the words on the page, starting with particular words like "bombardment" and "shelling." Are the words related? How do they know? If these two words and the word "trench" were erased from the text, what would be lost? As it happens, the whole of World War I is evoked in this little text by just those three words—and the larger context of the book in which they reverberate. If the words "Fossalta" and "Mestre" were lost from the text would this be important? Are these words as important as "bombardment," for instance? What does it mean to "go upstairs" with a girl at the Villa Rossa, anyway? How do we know? How important is it? What do we have to know about "Dear Jesus" to understand the story?

Such questions as those I have sketched out here constitute one way to initiate a discussion of what we do when we "read"— how we construct characters, situations, and a world out of words, by means of cultural codes and generic codes that enable us to process these words so as to construct from them a story.

Such discussion is one way in which students can understand their own production of *text within text*, but we should also find ways of allowing them to produce written texts that are *"within"* the world they have constructed by their reading. They should be invited to retell the story, to summarize it and to expand it. For instance, they might be asked to rewrite the story from the point of view of the girl at the Villa Rossa. What happened when this young man who had been frightened so badly "went up-stairs" with her? Did he swagger? Did he break down? Did he unburden himself of his fear? Was he like all the others or different in some way? In doing this I would encourage the students to think of Hemingway's text as a *version* of events that might indeed seem quite different from another perspective. From Hemingway's text they construct a story, and from their constructed story they produce another text, on the same level as Hemingway's. This writing is *within* Hemingway's base text because it accepts the outlines of the story as given in the original. If the student-writer wishes to modify a detail—say, allow the soldier to "tell" the girl something more than Heming-way indicates he told her—this can become a point of discussion. *Why* does the writer want to make this change?

Another possibility is to rewrite the story from the point of view of Jesus, which in this case would mean an omniscient view but with omniscience itself involved in the story. The soldier makes a promise to Jesus and breaks it, after all. Christian theology gives us clues as to how such an action by a human might be regarded by God. Writing from this point of view, the student would have to decide whether the passing of the shelling "up the line" and the sparing of the soldier's life were simply random events or if they were functions of the divine will. Such considerations will not only lead students to consider their own religious beliefs but to ask what beliefs are implied by Heming-way's text. For instance, how does the story change if we as-sume, on the one hand, that the soldier was spared by chance and, on the other, that he was spared by divine intervention?

A final possibility is to rewrite the story from the soldier's point of view. I would propose first that the students be asked to describe the *minimal change* necessary to accomplish this. They will find that only one change is needed. The word "he" must be changed to "I" on the three occasions where it appears (call it three changes, if you like). In discovering how easy this revision is, our students will begin to see how close to a first person narrative Hemingway's text was in the first place. In fact, the first person works better than the third in one important respect. It agrees with the first person plural in the eighth sentence: "*We* went to work. . . ." In Hemingway's text the narrator seems to be another soldier in the trench during that sentence but to have intimate, even omniscient, knowledge of the first soldier's thoughts (the "he" of the story) and private deeds at all other times. This curious situation brings us to the verge of *interpretation* and *criticism*—which is to be expected. By making reading a conscious process through the production and discussion of texts within text, we open the way to these other textual dimensions. We shall return to the problem of person and point-of-view after we consider the basic pedagogy involved in teaching the *interpretation* and *criticism* of a little story like Interchapter VII.

THE TEACHING OF INTERPRETATION

A certain amount of interpretation may be necessary to provide the cultural codes implicated in any story. Without some understanding of such institutions as the Christian Church, houses of prostitution, and trench warfare, the reader will have difficulty not just in interpreting but even in reading this text. One of the advantages of group study, as opposed to private consumption, of a text is that many interpretive obstacles to reading can be resolved by discussion in class or by group research where it is necessary. But these functions are only interpretation in the service of reading; they are not interpretation proper, which is the thematizing of a text. In thematizing a fictional text we move from the level of the specific events narrated—the soldier in the trench and at the Villa Rossa—to a more general level of social types and ethical values.

To help students develop interpretive skills Hemingway is especially useful for two reasons. First, he works with strong, simple values for the most part; and, second, he provides extremely little thematic commentary. That is, his values are not too subtle for beginning students to understand, but he rarely provides thematic formulas within his texts. Abstraction, generalization, thematicization—all these are left to the reader. The text narrates and describes but seldom comments. Yet the values are strongly present. We shall be examining the thematics of several short pieces, including Interchapter VII, but before turning to the specifics it will be necessary to provide some general advice about the pedagogy of interpretation. The great danger here is the instructor's temptation to show off, which is mirrored by the critic's temptation to do the same thing. (I am fighting it myself on every page here.) This is not simply a matter of vanity. There is a bright little student inside most teachers, who wants to set the rest of the class straight, because he or she *knows* the "right answer." Still, the point of teaching interpretation is not to usurp the interpreter's role but to explain the rules of the interpretive game, the code of interpretation as it is practiced within the institutional sedimentations that threaten to fossilize us all. These rules are common to all within the academic institution, as the rules of chess are common to all chess players. Therefore, we must teach the rules, and we must also teach the principles and procedures that lead to strong interpretive positions. In the world of chess, this means playing over important games, seeing how it has been done, always preparing for the moment when one confronts, alone, the unforeseen situation. In literary study, it means that interpretations should be read and studied along with the texts they interpret—not every time or all the time, but enough so that students can see how it is done and understand that it is never entirely done. An interpretive text is always in a network of relations with other texts and institutional practices. It is never a pure relation between a "primary" text and a single "secondary" text or commentary. Rather, it is a statement in a dialogue. To simplify the textual lives of our students, we may wish to "tune out" many of these voices, but the students should be aware that this is the case, and on some occasions they should be specifically invited to compose a text that knowingly enters the interpretive dialogue. The standard New Critical approach, you remember, allowed the instructor but not the students to tune in on the interpretive tradition, increasing the instructor's mysterious powers and the student's sense of powerlessness. By bringing the critical texts inside the classroom we make a greater textual power available to students. The point is not—as is sometimes charged—to substitute criticism for literature as the object of study but to make the object of study the whole intertextual system of relations that connects one text to others—a system that will finally include the student's own writing.

The teaching of interpretation—*text upon text*—must include the basic principles recognized by our institutional practice. That is, we need to equip our students with the accepted strategies for moving from following a narrative ("within") to thematizing one ("upon"). In terms of Interchapter VII, how should our students get from "It's about this soldier in a trench" to "It's about fear"—or shame, or betrayal, or hypocrisy, or human frailty, or whatever? All attempts to systematize this crucial step in the interpretive process (like the triangle of Lévi-Strauss or the rectangle of Greimas, recently adopted by Jameson) are vague if not downright deceptive about the genesis of their initial semantic oppositions. There is an element of intuition here, or, to be more precise, an instance of the mental process Charles Peirce called "abduction," that cannot be reduced to formulas. How, then, can the principles of interpretation be taught?

The problem is how we get from the things named in the story—character-things, situation-things, event-things—to the level of generalized themes and values. Sometimes a fictional text will "help" the reader by providing its own commentary, whether in the form of an Aesopian moral or some less blatant thematization. This dimension of a narrative text should be read as one reads an interpretive essay, but it need not be accepted as *the* interpretation of the narrative in which it is imbedded. "But," you may wish to ask, "doesn't the author know best?" Maybe, but what the author says can only be *read*. *Interpretation* lies on the other side of reading. Its domain is the unsaid: the implied, perhaps, or even the repressed.

In getting from the said and read to the unsaid and interpreted, we can use the assistance of the formalists and structuralists. The first things to look for are repetitions and oppositions that emerge at the obvious or manifest level of the text. Interchapter VII is such a little text that it does not afford much scope for interpretation, but it will enable us to make a start on exploring with our students the principles involved in thematizing a narrative. I would begin by reconsidering the reading of the story, inviting summaries and responses to questions about what makes it a story. I would do my best to keep such a discussion going until some of the following features emerged: that the story takes place in two locations, trench and Villa Rossa; that the soldier in the trench promises Jesus, in prayer, that he will tell about him, and that he breaks that promise first at the Villa Rossa and then for ever after. In such a discussion I would expect that certain cultural information important to the story would emerge. It is helpful to know that we are on the Italian front in World War I, and that undergoing an artillery bombardment in the trenches is a terrifying experience. The relevant bit of cultural coding was restated for World War II as "there are no atheists in fox holes"—the idea behind the gnomon being that the overwhelming proximity of death and destruction induces a religious experience. To read the story, we also need to know that Villa Rossa ("red house") was a generic name for the brothels provided for troops during that war, so that our soldier goes straight from his trench at Fossalta to the whore house back in Mestre. The forty-mile journey between the front lines and the city of Mestre (the railroad junction for Venice) is quite properly ignored by the story, which establishes a pattern based not on the difference between the two geographic locations but on the differences between "trench" and "Villa."

This opposition in the story—trench versus Villa—is the base upon which thematic oppositions are constructed. In leading a class from reading to interpretation, I would try to uncover the implications of the opposition by exploring all the relationships of similarity and difference that link the story's two main places and episodes. Like the protagonists in several of the stories in *In Our Time*, the soldier in Interchapter VII spends most of his time lying down. "He lay very flat and sweated" in the trench. Tell me, class, what did he do upstairs at the Villa Rossa? "He lay very flat and sweated"? Quite possibly. In the trench he speaks in personal, intimate terms to "dear Jesus." And in the Villa? We know less about the events in the Villa than the events in the trench, and this is a matter we shall have to consider when we turn from *interpretation* to *criticism*, but the textual pattern of oppositions is nevertheless very clear: not just trench against Villa but Jesus against "the girl" as well.

The next step is the crucial one. To accomplish it we must ask what these oppositions "represent," or as our institutional vocabulary usually phrases it, what they "symbolize." This is a difficult moment for teachers because this is the point at which our greater cultural information distances us from our students, enabling us to see patterns that are only dimly visible for many of them. This aspect of interpretation involves connecting the singular oppositions of the text to the generalized oppositions that structure our cultural systems of values. In other words, we are talking about ideology. Considered in this light, interpretation is not a pure skill but a discipline deeply dependent upon knowledge. It is not so much a matter of generating meanings out of a text as it is a matter of making connections between a particular verbal text and a larger cultural text, which is the matrix or master code that the literary text both depends upon and modifies. In order to teach the interpretation of a literary text, we must be prepared to teach the cultural text as well.

In the case of this tiny story, the textual oppositions we have emphasized must be connected to the larger cultural entities of which they may be seen as instances. Trench and Villa are tokens of the great cultural types, War and Love, whose iconography has been charted through countless images of Mars and Venus, and been embodied in countless literary characters. What is important in connecting Interchapter VII to this great cultural code or *topos* is that Hemingway has brought the icon down into the muck as far as he can. Venus is a hooker and Mars is a boy blubbering at the bottom of a trench. The act of interpretation involves both making the cultural connection (seeing the resemblance) and understanding the unique quality of this particular version of the larger instance (that is, noting the difference).

The oppositions in the text evoke another great cultural axis as well. Jesus and this Magdalene, the girl at the Villa Rossa, are drawn from another familiar repository of icons, the contrast between spirit and matter, between sacred and profane love. Images of prostitution are deeply imbedded in Christian religious lore and controversy, and the turn away from true religion to whore after strange gods or embrace the "Whore of Babylon" is a move of considerable cultural resonance. It is thus not difficult to see our soldier's trip to the Villa Rossa as a double betrayal: he abandons Jesus for the girl, and, like St. Peter, he does not bear witness as he promised. Once again, of course, it is enough to mention Peter's denial to note how Hemingway has debased this topic.

It is worth hazarding the view that the ultimate interpretation of this story must move from noting the cultural codes invoked to understanding the attitude taken toward those codes by the maker of this text. If religion is reduced to a frightened blubbering, quickly abandoned when fear is past, and love is debased to going upstairs at a bordello, then perhaps this reduction is itself a major theme of the text. Even war itself has been diminished here to its least heroic aspect: a frightened, defenseless creature pursued by relentless machines that spare his life only because their mechanical violence is randomly effective.

All these degradations become a thematic motif in Hemingway's larger text. To be in *"Our Time"* is to be in a world where human qualities are regularly crushed and brutalized by social and biological forces too powerful for individuals to resist. We have learned to call this attitude and the texts that embody it "naturalism," and to see it as a cultural code, arising at a particular point in human history. The interpretation of any single literary text, if pushed seriously, will lead us not to some uniquely precious exegetical act but to cultural history itself, which is of course a major part of our educational responsibility as teachers of literature. Such interpretation should also lead us to an awareness that interpretation is not only dependent upon a prior reading; it is also incomplete without a further extension into criticism.

THE TEACHING OF CRITICISM

Our presiding institution, the collectivity of academically sponsored scholars and teachers, is ill at ease with criticism. We prefer to leave that to the Samuel Johnsons or Edmund Wilsons, who may receive honorary doctorates but do not fit into our academic niches. We ourselves are more at home with interpretation, and we look askance at those of our number who seem to make too many value judgments—especially if they are severe ones. We were not comfortable with F. R. Leavis and Yvor Winters. Nor do we think it fitting that our students should have opinions about the merits of the masterpieces we dress and cook for their ingestion and admiration. Socrates, we might remember, once characterized rhetoricians as mere practitioners of a culinary art. Such a charge might be brought home more tellingly, even, to us.

How, then, can we honestly, legitimately, encourage our students to be critical—to produce *text against text*—in our literary classes? As I indicated earlier, criticism is not a matter of personal preference but of collective judgment. The critic must speak for a group or class on issues of importance to that class. In the case of Hemingway's Interchapter VII, the text is so small that there is as little room for criticism as there was for interpretation, but there is some. The story is about war and the kind of experiences to which people are subjected in war. But it gives us relatively extended treatment of what happens to a soldier and only the briefest possible mention of what happens to the "girl" who is serving as a prostitute during this war. She may have a relationship with Jesus Christ, too, but we will have to invent it ourselves if we want it in the story. It is a man's story, then, a soldier's story, but this means that we should at least open the question of whether Hemingway is a man's writer whose presence in a course should be balanced by a woman's writer. At any rate, a teacher of Hemingway should allow this sexual question to be introduced and allow female students in particular to indicate whether or not they feel excluded in some way from the concerns of this story and other stories in *In Our Time*. To whom does the "Our" refer, anyway?

If the stories open up "extratextual" concerns about prostitution and war, and the cultural sanctioning of these institutions, we teachers should not cut off such discussion as nonliterary but welcome it as recognizing a major function of written texts: the rendering of "accounts" that are themselves abstractions from the cultural text, versions of social reality for our consideration. So let us consider. One of the things our cultural interpretation might have led us to perceive is the way this little story follows an archetypal pattern, moving from down at the bottom of a trench to the trip "upstairs" at the Villa Rossa: from a modern inferno to a debased paradiso. Like Dante himself, our traveling soldier is led up by a woman. (You are thinking, I hope, that this is exactly the kind of show-off stuff that we should be avoiding. You are right; it is dangerous, and above all it should not be pushed. I would especially advise staying away from the words concealed in Fossalta and Mestre.) The down-to-up movement is very basic to the story. The allusion to Dante is not essential, though I think it provides a certain textual pleasure for the knowing reader. But the physical down-to-up movement is accompanied by a moral up-to-down movement from Jesus to the prostitute, or from the culturally sanctioned activity of war to the culturally disapproved activity of prostitution.

Our critical activity here must note that Hemingway has presented both war and prostitution as part of the way things are in our time. They are both, in fact, sanctioned by a culture that pretends to approve only of one. The disparity between what society claims to value and what it actually produces is a theme in some of Hemingway's stories in this volume, but it is not an explicit theme here. This is "neutral," "objective," "camera-eye" reporting—or it presents itself as such.

As critics we need to confront both the naturalistic attitude—this is the way things are, people can't help themselves—and the objective detachment of the narration—this is the way things happen, I am just recording. That is, the critic must ask why Hemingway himself assumes the positions of naturalism and objectivity, and what the consequences of such positions are in the world of human action. We should also question the source of this apparent indifference and objectivity. You will remember that in reading and rewriting this text we came upon the curious grammatical shift from third person—"he lay very flat"—to first person—"we went to work." This combination is curious because it seems to mark the narrator as *another* soldier in the trench who nevertheless hears the private prayers and pillow talk of the first soldier. One of these two soldiers does not tell "anybody" about this experience—ever. The other tells everybody, including us. We also noticed in our reading how easy it would be to rewrite the story in the first person. If this were done, it would make the story a confession, a telling at last of previously untold sins. And perhaps that is what it is.

This Interchapter follows immediately after "A Very Short Story" in *In Our Time*—a work I discussed at some length in chapter 7 of *Semiotics and Interpretation*.[2] As it happens, "A Very Short Story" was originally begun in the first person and then rewritten in the third. This change is a grammatical mark of the larger process of objectification that is represented in these stories. In many of them painful personal experiences were rewritten, distanced, objectified, so that they could function as modernist works of art. This combination of naturalism and aestheticism, so characteristic of Hemingway and the other major figures of modern fiction since Flaubert, has been the subject of considerable critical debate, ever since the powerful attacks on aestheticism and naturalism made by George Lukács in the thirties and forties (see the essays collected in *Writer and Critic*, for instance).

I am suggesting that at some level, in some way, our students must be invited into these critical debates, that they must see naturalism and aestheticism not simply as styles or modes of production in an isolated realm of "art," but as world views with social consequences. What this means in practical terms is that we must make available in the most efficacious form some of this critical controversy itself. The ability to criticize is a function of critical maturity. It must be earned by study and thought. We cannot expect our students to find it easy or do it very well at first. But we must start them on this path of development by showing them critics in action and encouraging them to produce their own critical texts—not always and inevitably "against," but taking a stand outside the values and attitudes that have been identified as Hemingway's by reading and interpretation. Criticism is "against" other texts insofar as it resists them in the name of the critic's recognition of her or his own values.

3

THE TEXT IN THE CLASS · II

> The reader finds his freedom (i) in decid-
> ing how to activate one or another of the
> textual levels and (ii) in choosing which
> codes to apply.
>
> Umberto Eco,
> *The Role of the Reader*

The process we have been examining is the pedagogy of textual power: the ways in which teachers can help students to recognize the power texts have over them and assist the same students in obtaining a measure of control over textual processes, a share of textual power for themselves. In working through the stages of reading, interpretation, and criticism, we move from a submission to textual authority in reading, through a sharing of textual power in interpretation, toward an assertion of power through opposition in criticism. This process is also based upon a continually widening concept of text, moving from a specific set of printed signs to the codes and modes of thought and value that enable those signs to bear meaning.

The initial submission is important. If we do not postulate the intentions of another subjectivity—call that subjectivity "Hemingway" in this case—behind the verbal text, we will never be able to reach the third or critical stage in this process. If we simply project our own subjective modes of thought and desire upon the text, our reading will never be sufficiently *other* for us to interpret it and, especially, to criticize it. We must assume authority and intentionality in reading, as E. D. Hirsch has been

arguing for years—though not, as Hirsch would have it, in order
to recover the only "valid" meaning in a text. We will have to go
a little deeper into this question of intentionality later on in this
chapter. For the moment it will be enough to note that the
reading of intentions is an important aspect of textual power: it
is important when a football quarterback "reads" a defense or a
constitutional lawyer examines a precedent. Wherever intentionality is assumed to exist, it presides over the act of reading—
as a teleological assumption, however, rather than as a method
or solution to the problem of understanding. It is, after all, only
an *aspect* of textual power—an aspect which dominates the
reading of human texts for a very good reason. Without a serious
act of "reading"—of a book, a face, or a tone of voice—we will
never be able to agree or disagree with another person, since we
will have turned all others into mirrors of ourselves. Reading—
as a submission to the intentions of another—is the first step in
all thought and all communication. It is essential; but it is incomplete in itself. It requires both interpretation and criticism for
completion.

We move from *reading* to *interpretation* by questioning that
very unity of subjectivity and intention that we have postulated
in order to read. We do this by exploring the cultural codes
invoked by the producer of a text and by looking for signs of
counter-intentionality, division of purpose, the return of the
repressed, in the text before us. Hirsch's theory of interpretation
founders on the rock of psychic unity, an assumption thoroughly
discredited by theoreticians from Freud to Derrida. It would be
an astonishing thing if an extended body of written work did not
reveal signs of divided consciousness—as if everyday life had no
psychopathology, and civilization no discontents. In some other
world, perhaps, but not in ours can such a state of affairs prevail.

The move from *interpretation* to *criticism* is not simply a
destructive negation, however, not a mere rejection of ideas and
values proposed by a text. It is a differentiation of the subjectivity of the critic from that of the author, an assertion of *another*
textual power against that of the primary text. Even agreement

is significant only if the critic's subjectivity is differentiated from the author's. The attempt to encourage or "teach" this kind of textuality is of course fraught with difficulty. It may easily drift into the ridiculous pose of an indoctrination in freedom, an attempt to "program" or condition people to behave independently. Obviously, this is not the way to go. The first step toward any kind of critical independence is the study of constraint. This is one reason why the submission involved in reading is important. A student needs to feel the power of a text, to experience the pleasures obtainable only through submission, before he or she can begin to question both that pleasure and its requisite submission. Criticism begins with the recognition of textual power and ends in the attempt to exercise it. This attempt may take the form of an essay, but it may just as easily be textualized as a parody or countertext in the same mode as its critical object. As teachers, we should encourage the full range of critical practice in our students.

We can return now to *In Our Time*, the text I have proposed for an illustration of the ways in which textual power can be studied. Let us begin with "The Revolutionist," a little sketch of eight paragraphs in length, not much longer than some of the Interchapters. (In the first publication, *in our time*, it was on the same level as the others.) I call it a sketch rather than a story because, as the title suggests, it concentrates on character rather than event: not the revolution but the revolutionist. (Once again, I must ask the reader to begin by obtaining a copy of the text.)

READING "THE REVOLUTIONIST"

With sketches like this it is almost always useful to begin by asking how much of a story the text presents. There is, in fact, a little narrative to be constructed from this text: the story of a young man who has been imprisoned for the political cause of revolution, and apparently tortured by "Horthy" and the "Whites" in his native Hungary, but who has come to Italy with his revolutionary faith and joy in life undiminished; this story

ends with him in prison once again, but in Switzerland where the
conditions should be better. Having observed all that, we can see
how this text is more interested in character than in plot, though
this "character," since it is embedded in the story of a change
that is only partly a change, from a bad prison to a good one—
this "character" must in some way explain the story and be
explained or illustrated by it.

In reading this text as a sketch of character, students should
be invited to list and discuss the adjectives that are associated
with the pronoun "he" in the text. Character, after all, is something the reader constructs from the connotations of the words
associated with a recurring proper name or—as so often in *In
Our Time*—a pronoun. "He" is "shy," "young," "nice," and
"eager." He is also "very" and "quite." That is, he is "*very* shy,"
"*quite* young," "*very* nice," and "*very* eager." Perhaps even
more than the adjectives, the adverbs function here to convey
the quality of the revolutionist's character. I would certainly
encourage my students to characterize this young man themselves, in their own words, avoiding Hemingway's verbal formulas as much as possible. I would also encourage them to characterize the text's other pronoun: "I."

In describing "I" they will have only the indirect clues of the
text to go on, but these should be enough. The best possible
writing assignment designed to elicit *text within text* from this
story would be a double task. Describe "I" as the revolutionist
himself might have described him (to a fellow prisoner or Red
Cross nurse in Sion, for example), and then describe him again
("I," that is), as you, the reader, understood him. These two
descriptions should differ sufficiently to open the way toward
interpreting the text, for the meaning of this text must be sought
in the basic opposition embodied in the characters of the describ*er* and the describ*ee*, "I" and "he," as presented through
the medium of Hemingway's prose.

INTERPRETING "THE REVOLUTIONIST"

We can begin with what I have called interpretation in the
service of reading. This little text is unusually dependent on

cultural codes, without which only a very impoverished reading can be managed. Two cultural domains are especially prominent: politics and history, on the one hand, and aesthetics and art history, on the other. There are two reasonable ways to deal with this knowledge, depending on the time available—either to send students to the library or to provide it as a handout.

In the political and historical domain, information will center on the place and date of the major action, the north of Italy in "early September," 1919, and the immediately preceding events in Hungary. Students need to know enough to identify or explain the words "Whites," "Budapest," "Magyar," "Horthy." I would want them to know also what is implied in the phrase "in spite of Hungary." There is simply no way around a little lesson in geography, history, and politics here, nor should we want to get around it. This is one of the things that literary study is *for*: it opens the way to a critique of culture.

Having learned something of the August 1919 counterrevolution in Hungary and the "White Terror" led by Admiral Horthy, students will be able to place Hemingway's Magyar boy—"The Revolutionist"—as one of the thousands of Hungarians imprisoned, tortured, and exiled by "Horthy's men." A reference to George Lukács's reflections on his own thoughts and feelings at the time can also be illuminating (see especially the preface to *History and Class Consciousness*),[1] not only for the events in Hungary but also for Italian politics. When the young Magyar asks the narrator about how "the movement" is going in Italy, he is asking about that "wave of revolution" that Lukács and many other revolutionists believed "would soon sweep the whole world" (*HCC*, p. xiii). The narrator, who is also clearly in "the movement," says that things are going badly in Italy. The revolutionist says that "it will go better. . . . You have everything here. It is the one country everyone is sure of. It will be the starting point of everything." How are we to understand these words? Only, I should think, in the light of what actually happened—that is, the events culminating in Mussolini's seizure of power in 1923. Walter L. Adamson, in *Hegemony and Revolution*, comments that "the revolutionary moment which existed in Italy above all in 1919 was missed, and the groundwork was laid for a powerful right-wing reaction."[2] Hemingway has poised his story at exactly the "revolutionary moment," the moment when the socialist left lost control and the way was prepared for the rise of a nationalistic fascism. Writing in 1923, Hemingway was aware of the abrupt end that had come to revolutionary hopes in Italy. He himself had been back home in Illinois in September of 1919. History, not personal experience, dictated the timing of this little sketch. And history, of course, by 1923 had already made the Revolutionist's optimism as ironic as his journey from jail to jail.

The historical coding of this story is given color and nuance by another body of information, drawn from Italian art. It is quite remarkable that in a story about a revolutionist, a sketch less than 400 words long, we should encounter the names of Giotto, Masaccio, and Piero della Francesca. It is even more remarkable that we should encounter the name of a fourth painter—Andrea Mantegna—not once but three times. The narrator and the revolutionist are in total disagreement about two things in this text: the future of the movement in Italy and their feelings about Mantegna's art. The revolutionist's reaction to Mantegna is obviously significant to the narrator and to Hemingway, for it is reported in two phrases of startling symmetry: "Mantegna he did not like" and "he did not like Mantegna." Why not? And why is it important? As we move from reading to interpretation, we can see that the values in this story are organized around the opposition between the narrator and the revolutionist, which are in turn dependent upon such matters as their attitudes toward the revolution and toward Mantegna or the relative talkativeness of the revolutionist ("He talked about it a little") and taciturnity of the narrator ("I did not say anything"). The passivity or "patiency" of the revolutionist (he is imprisoned, tortured, exiled, "passed on" by the train men, taken into the Romagna, told where to eat, and finally imprisoned again) is also contrasted with the activity or "agency" of the narrator, who goes "to see a man," writes out "the addresses of comrades," suggests a visit to the "Mantegnas in Milano," and, finally, tells the story we are reading.

At this point in our interpretation, the only mystery is Mantegna. This is another place where the students need outside information in order to discuss the way the four painters figure in "The Revolutionist." Among other things, it should probably be noted that Hemingway's narrator has mentioned them in strict chronological order: Giotto, Masaccio, Piero della Francesca, Mantegna. Taken as a sequence, they might illustrate the growing mastery of illusionary technique in the Italian renaissance, especially the increasing concern for visual perspective in representation—but other painters could have been used for this. The more the problem is considered, the more obvious it becomes that Mantegna has a special meaning for this narrator—and perhaps for Hemingway—that must extend beyond aesthetics and technique. All four painters worked mainly with religious themes. It might be possible to say that Mantegna was more preoccupied with martyrdom and hence with torture than the others, but they all painted scenes from the passion of Christ, for instance. There is a clue, perhaps, in the mention of "Mantegnas in Milano." Many of the finest Mantegnas were in Padua, where they were later destroyed in World War II, but in 1919, as at the present time, there was only one notable Mantegna in Milan—a virtuoso perspective view of the dead Christ, a greenish corpse laid out with his wounds highly visible: very human and very dead.

One could argue without further evidence that the naturalism of this painting must have appealed powerfully to the naturalist in Hemingway, who had ample opportunity to see this work when he was hospitalized and convalescent in Milan in 1918. But there *is* further evidence (as Kenneth G. Johnston, in particular, has pointed out in an article called "Hemingway and Mantegna: The Bitter Nail Holes").[3] There is evidence, at any rate, that throws considerable light on what Mantegna stood for in Hemingway's code. This evidence is to be found in passages from two of Hemingway's novels: *A Farewell to Arms* and *For*

Whom the Bell Tolls.[4] (I would suggest introducing the passages into classroom discussion only *after* students have worried the meaning of "Mantegna" a bit without this evidence. There is a crucial interpretive principle involved here, to which we shall be attending.) Here are the passages:

> "Do you know anything about art?"
> "Rubens," said Catherine.
> "Large and fat," I said.
> "Titian," Catherine said.
> "Titian-haired," I said. "How about Mantegna?"
> "Don't ask hard ones," Catherine said. "I know him though—very bitter."
> "Very bitter," I said. "Lots of nail holes."
> [*A Farewell to Arms* (1929), chapter 37]

At either of those places you felt that you were taking part in a crusade. That was the only word for it although it was a word that had been so worn and abused that it no longer gave its true meaning. You felt, in spite of all bureaucracy and inefficiency and party strife something that was like the feeling you expected to have and did not have when you made your first communion. It was a feeling of consecration to a duty toward all of the oppressed of the world which would be as difficult and embarrassing to speak about as religious experience and yet it was authentic as the feeling you had when you heard Bach, or stood in Chartres Cathedral or the Cathedral at León and saw the light coming through the great windows; or when you saw Mantegna and Greco and Brueghel in the Prado. It gave you a part in something that you could believe in wholly and completely and in which you felt an absolute brotherhood with the others who were engaged in it. It was something that you had never known before but that you had experienced now and you gave such importance to it and the reasons for it that your own death seemed of complete unimportance; only a thing to be avoided because it would interfere with the performance of your duty. But the best thing was that there was something you could do about this feeling and this necessity too. You could fight. [*For Whom the Bell Tolls* (1940), chapter 18]

A DIGRESSION ON "INTENTION"

The principle at stake in bringing these Mantegna passages to bear upon "The Revolutionist" has been most frequently presented in terms of authorial "intention." Presumably the New Critics, led by Wimsatt and Beardsley, would have to argue that to consider these passages from the novels as keys to meaning in the short story would be an egregious instance of the intentional fallacy, while the New Critics' nemesis, E. D. Hirsch, would argue that the passages in question are precious revelations of authorial intention, which is in turn vital in arriving at the "valid" meaning of any text. We, as teachers, may or may not wish to trouble our students about this theoretical dispute, but we will have to make up our minds about our own positions in it, simply in order to decide whether to make this material available or to conceal it.

My position is that the debate, as it has been developed— between a view that holds authorial intention irrelevant and an opposed view that authorial intention is decisive—admits of no resolution. It does not even allow for any acceptable intermediate position. The whole problem of the supports or guides for textual meaning must be seen in terms other than the authority of the author or the freedom of the reader. Both of these notions will have to be abandoned, as will the crucial New Critical position that the text authorizes its own meaning and controls all readings. The missing ingredient in all these formulations is the cultural system in which all of these individualities—the writer, the reader, and the text—take shape and have their being. All individuals attain their subjectivity by mastering cultural and symbolic codes—and by being mastered in turn by the codes they acquire. The writer, the reader, and the text—all are coded: by language, the most comprehensive code, and by other social and institutional systems that can be described and understood in terms of the notion of code. With this in mind, let us reconsider the question of "intention," beginning with the situation of the reader of any text. A text is always read by a historical person, a person, that is, located at a specific point in a cultur-

al tradition. This actual person—you, me, our student—tries
(should try, must try) to decode the signs that constitute the text
by connecting those signs to the semantic fields that are appropriate to them. The appropriate fields must be those that were
operative at the time of the production of the text, operative for
its producer. *Reading* is possible only to the extent that the
actual reader shares a semantic and syntactic field with the
writer. A "field" in this sense is a set of codes and paradigms that
enable and constrain meaning. The further estranged the reader
is from the writer (by time, space, language, or temperament)
the more *interpretation* must be called upon to provide a conscious construction of unavailable or faded codes and paradigms. If we are going to read John Donne, for example, we
must recover something of the codes of alchemy, Neoplatonism,
Petrarchan erotics, early Anglican theology, and a feeling for
the syntax and semantics of a spoken and written English vastly
different from our own.

    In every code or syntactic-semantic field there is much that is
historical and collective and some small but possibly important
part that is unique and individual. In Hemingway's use of the
word "Mantegna" we have a beautiful example of the intersec-
tion of a private or individual code and the public codes of
history and culture. Andrea Mantegna belongs to the history of
art, but he also belongs to Hemingway in some special way that
forces us out of the mode of reading and into that of a "submissive" interpretation. Interpretation, as Fredric Jameson has
pointed out, citing Paul Ricoeur as his model (*The Political
Unconscious*, pp. 284–85; *Freud and Philosophy*, pp. 26–27),
has two modes, negative and positive—"willingness to suspect,
willingness to listen: vow of obedience, vow of rigor" (*PU*, p.
284; *FP*, p. 27). In the system I am developing here, interpretation, when it looks toward reading, is in the positive mode, the
mode of listening and obedience; when it looks toward criticism,
however, interpretation is in the negative mode, the mode of
suspicion and rigor.

    "Intention" is a fiction, a heuristic device of the obedient or positive mode of interpretation. Postulating an intention is a way of "listening." Intentionality can never settle or validate a meaning because there can never be a pure manifestation of intentionality. That is, we will never find Hemingway's intention in any form that transcends textuality; and every text requires reading, interpretation, and criticism. We settle our notion of Hemingway's meaning and Hemingway's intention to mean *at the same moment*, and we can do this only by assuming that a unified Hemingway intended a unified meaning in the first place.

In discussing Ricoeur's theory, Jameson argues that it is limited by "the persistence of categories of the individual subject." In particular, he objects to the way that Ricoeur's notion of positive meaning "is modeled on the act of communication between individual subjects, and cannot therefore be appropriated as such for any view of meaning as a collective process" (*PU*, p. 285). If Jameson is looking for a purely collective kind of meaning he is pursuing a *fata morgana*. It is a given, an *a priori* of the linguistic horizon, if you like, that linguistic encoding and decoding is done by specific historical individuals. This is one of the constituent features of interpretation. It is also a given, however, that the social, the cultural, the collective, and the historical sedimentations of tradition provide the inescapable media and codes for human exchanges of meaning. Interpretation must, always and inevitably, deal with individuals in their historical specificity and also with the irreducibly collective dimensions of language and culture. Moreover, as we move from positive to negative interpretation, and on to criticism, as I have already argued in chapter 2, we move from assumptions of individuality and unity to assumptions of disunity and collectivity. We can criticize only as representatives of a group or class. To the extent that individuals are indeed "subjects," constituted by transindividual codes, both biological and cultural, the notion of "individual subject" is itself paradoxical.

To sum up, authorial intention is at best a requirement of reading and therefore a partial goal of interpretation, rather

than a key that unlocks valid meanings. As a goal of pedagogy it
seems to me better to emphasize the reconstruction of codes that
organize meaning than to insist on reaching the goal of some
"one right reading" of a text. We have already considered how
the public and historical events in Hungary and Italy from 1918
to 1923 are an indispensable code for understanding "The Revolutionist." Now we must consider how the cultural placement of
Mantegna has been modified by the private idiolect of the individual Ernest Hemingway. We must do this for many reasons,
one of them being our human urge to know, to get to the bottom
of things, but another reason is that we need to position Hemingway as an Other, a distinct subjectivity, in order to criticize him
and define ourselves against him.

INTERPRETING "THE REVOLUTIONIST" (continued)

Let us reconsider the two "Mantegna" passages from the
novels. One of them was written five or six years after "The
Revolutionist" and the other perhaps an additional ten years
later. Neither could tell us anything "valid" about Hemingway's
intentions at the moment of writing "The Revolutionist." I am
going to argue, however, that all three passages taken together
reveal a pattern or paradigm that is a persistent feature of the
subjectivity we call "Ernest Hemingway." It is this very kind of
persistence, in fact, which is the principal external evidence for
that subjective continuity we recognize as the "same" human
being. Certainly, one of our goals as teachers should be to show
our students how one goes about understanding a writer. This is
a basic tool of scholarship, and its usefulness extends well beyond academic life. One feature of this process is that the interpreter must read as widely as possible in a writer's texts, so as to
learn, tacitly or explicitly, the writer's idiolect, the writer's personal coloration of the codes with which he or she works. (This
is, for instance, a conspicuous part of Derrida's method in his
commentary on Husserl's "Origin of Geometry.") In our hypo-
thetical introductory course, we cannot expect our students to

read widely in any single author, but the process can at least be enacted by a teacher who has read widely and makes the fruits of this reading available to the class for their use, rather than hoarding them up to enrich some superior, teacherly display.

The three "Mantegna" passages in Hemingway's writing (the only three I have found so far) share a number of interesting features. In every case, Mantegna is mentioned in connection with other artists, which is not surprising. But he is always mentioned as the equivalent or superior to other artists who are perhaps better known. In every case his name is introduced by a male narrator in a situation of some stress. The situations have a surprising amount in common. In *A Farewell to Arms*, Frederic and Catherine discuss painters just after escaping from Italy to Switzerland, where they have been arrested and detained. In *For Whom the Bell Tolls*, Robert Jordan is sitting in a cave, thinking about how to perform his demolition job and escape the fascists. He is a revolutionist, of sorts, himself; certainly he is a fervent socialist, as the passage before us indicates. He is meditating on two places in embattled Madrid, places that are very different in atmosphere but united by a collective ideal that provides a transfiguring experience, a political experience that is for Jordan the only truly religious experience he has known: "it was like the feeling you expected to have and did not have when you made your first communion." He describes the feeling as *authentic*, a critical word, and likens it to the experience of the greatest art: music (Bach), architecture (the cathedrals of Chartres and León), painting (Mantegna, El Greco, and Brueghel). All these artists produce the same authentic feeling that Jordan associates with "consecration to a duty toward all of the oppressed of the world."

If "authentic" is the word for Mantegna in this passage, "bitter" is the word for him in the other novel. Compared with those later glorifiers of flesh and fabric, Rubens and Titian, Mantegna stands out as the painter of the *corpus Christi*, the body of a dead man, waiting for resurrection. The appearance of Mantegna in all three works comes a little before the bitter end: the failure of revolution and arrest of the revolutionist in *In Our Time*, the death of Catherine in *A Farewell to Arms*, the death of Jordan and the fall of Spain to the fascists in *For Whom the Bell Tolls*. Some of these ends are "in" the texts and some are "outside" or "beyond" them, but it would be a lunatic perversion of New Critical thought to ignore the code of history that surrounds these three texts.

In attempting to understand the "value" or meaning of "Mantegna" in Hemingway's textual system, we have uncovered a portion of a paradigmatic system that links socialism and authenticity with bitterness and failure. Is this Hemingway's private pessimism, or is it simply the expression of history itself, speaking through an individual who tried to hold art and politics together so that history *could* speak through him and inform his texts? Can we even make this kind of question available to our students in an introductory course? We will never know unless we make the attempt. But there is so much to learn here, about history, politics, art, and perhaps even life, that we owe it to our profession, and our own hopes for the future of the world, to try.

Returning to "The Revolutionist" we can see how Mantegna represents the narrator's world view, a bitter pessimism that does not prevent him from going "to see a man," doing revolutionary work he is too discreet to describe. He is sustained, perhaps, like Robert Jordan, by the authenticity of texts that can transmute mere bitterness into art: texts like Mantegna's dead Christ and perhaps like Hemingway's stories, too. In "The Revolutionist" the narrator is astonishingly persistent in his attempt to interest the young Magyar in Mantegna's painting, and astonishingly persistent in telling us about it, too. He seems to feel that we *need* to experience Mantegna. If being tortured by Horthy's men was not enough to turn this Magyar "boy" into a "man"—and it is clear from the text that the narrator considers him a "boy"—perhaps Mantegna can provide the necessary rite of passage. Or perhaps Hemingway, for us.

In teaching the interpretation of this story, I would certainly ask my students to comment on the image of the young Magyar carrying reproductions of Giotto, Masaccio, and Piero della Francesca, "wrapped in a copy of *Avanti*." Knowing that the three artists were mainly religious painters of the transition from the later Middle Ages to the Renaissance, they will still need to know that *Avanti* is the Italian word for "forward" and is the name of a newspaper. Actually, the title of the newspaper included an exclamation mark: *Avanti!* It was, like other journalistic efforts carrying the title "Forward!" in other tongues and countries, the organ of a socialist party, in this case the PSI, the Italian Socialist Party. Mussolini had been its editor, before he abandoned socialism. Gramsci had written for it. In April of 1919 its offices were destroyed by fascist violence, but in September a young revolutionist might still have been reading it. He might not, however, be expected to use it as wrapping for religious reproductions.

Forward! to the utopian future on the outside; back toward the Middle Ages on the inside. Dialectical materialism on the outside; theological spiritualism on the inside. This image embodies the kind of binary oppositions that interpretation seeks to reveal as the axes of value in a text. In the classroom, students should be encouraged to unpack this symbolism and to consider how the interpreter moves from the specific fact—say Giotto's paintings of the life of Jesus, wrapped in an issue of *Avanti!*—to the abstract level of past versus future or religion versus politics. One should also raise the issue of how these oppositions are mapped onto the more structural opposition of "inside" versus "outside." This can be done by raising the question of how one would interpret the image if *Avanti!* were concealed *inside* some reproductions by Giotto or Piero della Francesca. Since interpretation necessarily concerns itself with manifest and latent meaning, interpreters must inevitably privilege arrangements that emphasize insides and outsides. Having come this far, we are in a position to raise a further question. How can the interpreter finally get "outside" the power of a text and effect the transition from interpretation to criticism? Where does the negative hermeneutic begin and how should it proceed?

CRITICIZING "THE REVOLUTIONIST"

This is not an easy text on which to get a critical purchase, but the binary opposition between an immature optimism and a mature pessimism is probably the place to start. What is missing is any middle term, a character like George Lukács himself, perhaps, who at the moment of this story's action was beginning his self-critique and the long struggle to bring the revolution back to Hungary. The world Hemingway gives us here has a terrible bleakness, which is underlined by the irony of the last word of the text. The Revolutionist is imprisoned near "Sion," the Swiss-French town named for the hill of Zion in Jerusalem, remembered with so much pain by the Psalmist in captivity, and the very symbol of every exile's desire for the homeland. This kind of exquisite irony on the part of fate (and the author, of course) is characteristic of literary naturalism, which almost always proffers an unearned pessimism, in that the writer is much better off than the characters whose entrapment he is lovingly presenting.

Hemingway never worked for socialism in Italy as his narrator does in this story. He was safe at home in September, 1919, a wounded hero whose problems were strictly personal and domestic. But he did work for socialism in Spain during the Civil War, and in the character of Robert Jordan he filled in the motivational blank behind the narrator of "The Revolutionist." The naturalistic pessimism of "The Revolutionist" is to some extent redeemed by texts like the Mantegna passage from *For Whom the Bell Tolls* (quoted above). The transfiguring experience of a social "crusade" validates Jordan's life and makes his death and even the loss of the war bearable because the struggle has been meaningful and will continue. The pessimism of "The Revolutionist" is also redeemed to some extent by history itself. The narrator may in fact be seen simply as a realist in a hopeless position. Criticism is finally reduced to arguing that the Magyar is too much a cartoon figure, too extreme an example of invincible Panglossian joy. To this one can only reply that it hasn't prevented critics from seeing him as a heroic figure of resilience in adversity. Such a reading, of course, is itself Panglossian, cheerfully ignoring or repressing much that less happy readers can scarcely ignore.

What is missing is not simply a middle term, halfway between optimism and pessimism. What is missing is self-reflective thought: in a word, "criticism." It is worth noting that this is missing in *For Whom the Bell Tolls*, too. In that novel—as we can see even in the single paragraph on socialism, art, religion, and authenticity that we have before us because the name "Mantegna" appears in it—Hemingway does a good job of conveying an emotion that valorizes the socialist position of his protagonist. But he does this by putting religion, aesthetics, and politics on exactly the same level: the level of feeling. It is this move to the aesthetic and the sensational, so characteristic of the modern novelists, that is at the heart of Hemingway's power. It is at once his strength and his weakness. He makes us see, hear, and feel strongly. But everything he does, all his aesthetic choices, lead us away from sustained thought. Perhaps this is why a bullfight is as suitable an object of contemplation for him as a revolution or a war. To see this is to ask whether history is, as it sometimes seems, the subtext of a story like "The Revolutionist," or only a pretext for an essentially ahistorical, uncritical contrast between amateur and professional, or boy and man.

Establishing a critical perspective is especially hard for students, whose own thoughts and values are likely to be constantly wavering and far from clear. It may be that something as simple as asking where their sympathies lie in this story—with "he" or "I"—will serve as a point of departure for a growing critical awareness, if, at the same time the question of where "Hemingway's" sympathies lie is considered. The aim of this kind of teaching is not some definitive evaluation of this little sketch or of Hemingway as a writer, but the development of a critical awareness that comes from situating oneself over here, as against "Hemingway" over there—a thing that students in a class must do individually by negotiating interpretations and judgments with the others in their group. The teacher's role is not to settle the rightness or wrongness of these individual acts of criticism, but to interact, to negotiate, and to make available the critical positions already on record, where and when they will be useful. It is also the teacher's job to provide the analytical tools that will help students penetrate the clever surface of texts like these so that criticism may begin.

One such tool is the traditional, formal consideration of "point of view." In "The Revolutionist" the mature comrade is not simply set in opposition to the boy; he sets himself in opposition. He is the narrator, addressing some narratee in a conversational style, from "In 1919 he was travelling" to "the last I heard of him." It is the narrator who has ended this text with the ironic flourish of "in jail near Sion." He is taking a storyteller's pleasure in exposing a character he chooses to call a "Revolutionist." Why? What is his motive? If he is mocking, why does he mock? Is it a cover for his own bitterness at the failure of revolution? Why does *he* tell the story as I? In a number of these stories (such as Interchapter VII and "A Very Short Story") we find a text that seems made for first person narration told, with some difficulty, in the third person. Here we have a story totally removed from Hemingway's own experience told in the first person—producing a telling that calls into question its own motivation. Why does this happen?

The formalist explanation, which has actually been proposed, is that Hemingway was learning his craft, experimenting with point of view in these texts. There is no reason to doubt this, but there are other determinants involved in some of his choices. Many of these have to do with what is a major problem for Hemingway, a problem that will enable criticism to get a firmer grip on *In Our Time*, if we seek it in a somewhat more ambitious textual configuration than "The Revolutionist." The problem involves the relationship between action and passion, agency and patiency, and the complex dynamic between this active/passive relationship and another: the relationship between observing and being observed, between telling and being told about, between writing and being written. The final question in this problematic will involve the status of writing itself. Is a reporter in the active or the passive role? Is he in history or outside of it? Is he fighting or has he made a separate peace? This problematic is beautifully displayed in the six bullfighting Interchapters (IX–XIV) of *In Our Time*, which we must now consider.

4

THE TEXT IN THE CLASS · III

> An ideological bias can lead a critical
> reader to make a given text say more
> than it apparently says, that is, to find
> out what in that text is ideologically pre-
> supposed, untold.
>
> Umberto Eco,
> *The Role of the Reader*

We often assume that the development of a curriculum is an
innocent occupation, for which we need accept no personal
responsibility. The "masterpieces" are *there*, so we teach them.
They have been pre-selected by culture, laid down like fossils in
the sedimented layers of institutional tradition. Our only duty is
to make them relevant, to make Shakespeare "our contemporary." As you might expect, I am critical of this position. It is
much more important, I should think, to try making ourselves
Shakespeare's contemporaries, for a while, if only because it is
better exercise for the critical imagination or, more importantly,
because without such attempts we lose history and become the
pawns of tradition. The curriculum must be subject to critical
scrutiny like everything else in our academic institutions. Its very
"naturalness," its apparent inevitability, makes it especially suspect.

I have been arguing for Hemingway's place in an elementary
English curriculum, if he is properly balanced by other writers,
for instance writers whose texts will be more appealing to female
students. To some people this may seem like a trivial issue, but it
is not. Hemingway has proved uninteresting or repellent to

women scholars as well as to undergraduate women. Jackson J. Benson's "Comprehensive Checklist" in *The Short Stories of Ernest Hemingway* shows, in the category of books on Hemingway's work containing discussions of his short stories, thirty by men and three by women, with three ambiguous (initials only). Even in the category of general books containing discussions of Hemingway stories, we find forty-eight by men and only one by a woman (again, with three ambiguous). This is a rough measure, admittedly, but the figures on Henry James, for instance, would be very different. The limited sexual range of Hemingway's appeal is a real, historical phenomenon. "Masterpieces" have genders. They, too, are grounded in difference.

To justify teaching Hemingway we must make his sexual bias a part of our study, rather than pretend that the matter is inartistic and therefore extracurricular. The only woman who appears in the little sketches that I am considering here is the "girl" in the Villa Rossa. There are, in fact, more "girls" than women in *In Our Time*, which, again, is an aspect of them that must be included in any critical scrutiny of that book. One response to this situation is to ask whether, since Hemingway is offensive or uninteresting to women, there is any justification for teaching him at all. My answer to this question is that school is the one place where our major concern is to study what we don't know, to confront Otherness rather than to ignore it or convert it into a simulacrum of ourselves. But we must, indeed, confront and scrutinize this Otherness; we must criticize it. To some extent, it is Hemingway's fallibility that makes him so useful in the curriculum. Or rather, it is his combination of strength and weakness, his considerable rhetorical skill and formal control combined with a very disputable set of values: it is his humanity, if you will, that makes him interesting.

But his values *must* be confronted, especially as they function in stories that involve relationships between men and women. I do not intend to treat these stories here, primarily because (as I mentioned above, in chapter 2) I have already published an extended critique of one such text ("A Very Short

Story"); but I will use a brief excerpt from one of them to illustrate the kind of critical scrutiny I have in mind, before turning to the purely masculine world of Hemingway's bullfighting Interchapters. "Mr. and Mrs. Elliot" is a nasty and funny— one could almost say "bitchy"—story about a disastrous marriage that degenerates into a *ménage à trois*, in which the wife and her female friend sleep together while the husband engages in a kind of verbal masturbation, writing poetry all night and looking "very exhausted" in the morning. There are, in fact, strong hints that the masturbation is not purely verbal, such hints being part of the pervasive nastiness or bitchiness that gives the story is special quality. But this is not the place to attempt a full-scale critique of this text. I am going to take a few lines of it, only, to illustrate a pedagogical principle. In these lines we are given some information about Mr. Elliot:

> He wanted to keep himself pure so that he could bring to his wife the same purity of mind and body that he expected of her. He called it to himself living straight. He had been in love with various girls before he kissed Mrs. Elliot and always told them sooner or later that he had led a clean life. Nearly all the girls lost interest in him.

The humor of this depends upon the iterative quality of the experience described. Mr. Elliot keeps making the same mistake over and over again. His mistake, of course, is based upon a moral code that valorizes "straightness" or sexual innocence and denigrates sexual experience. It is, in fact, the code of all Christian sects and most other moral and religious systems. This code is held up to ridicule by being measured against another code, valorized by the text itself, the code of a worldly wisdom that grounds itself in "reference" and "truth." This code says that women may be accorded the place of innocence in American culture but, at bottom, they are sexual creatures and want only men who are sexually experienced enough to please them. Like all texts in the realistic/naturalistic mode, this one founds its authority upon reference (or pseudo-reference) to the real world. What women "really" want is confirmed by a kind of behavioral test or opinion poll: "Nearly all the girls" prefer what the text will call in the next sentence "rotters"—a term clearly derived from Mr. Elliot's discourse and carefully made ridiculous in context.

To appreciate the humor we must accept, at least provisionally, the cultural code of the text: its knowing leer and its opinion of "girls." If we want to be amused, if we want to be considered knowing, if we want to be successful with "girls" ourselves—we must snap at this bait. The alternative, as the rest of the text presents it, is to be the complacent husbands of lesbian wives. The assumed audience here is clearly male. But there is more in the passage before us than a merely masculine point of view. One of the things that makes Mr. Elliot ridiculous—when seen within the framework of Hemingway's sexual code—is his wish "that he could bring to his wife the same . . . that he expected of her." With the semantic burden of inexperience removed from this proposition, it does not look so silly from our present perspective on these matters. That is, precisely this sort of sexual equality is now a part of the cultural coding that constitutes many of us as subjects. We consider this sort of equality "natural." But, clearly, such views are not worldwide. And, just as clearly, they are not Hemingway's views either—at least they are not the views of the "Hemingway" we must construct in order to criticize this text. If we accept the textual pleasure proffered by the passage before us, if we enjoy this humor, we are in the text's power for as long as our pleasure lasts, and our codes are subordinated to those of the text. Only a critical act can free us from this power. An important part of the teacher's function in a literature classroom is to show students how to move from reading the text to interpreting and criticizing the codes that sustain the text's implications. Again and again we must stop and linger over passages like this one to ask, not simply whether our students "got it," but if they understand the exchange of pleasure and power involved in this particular act of "getting it." We have to keep asking, "What do you think of

that? Do you accept that?" But they must answer for themselves.

In the past we have often thought our jobs complete if our
students learned how to read or "understand." But even *Understanding Poetry* made some attempt at teaching criticism as
well—attempts which were notoriously unsuccessful, as in mis-
takenly treating a parody ("The Bells of Shandon") as a serious
poem, or in trying to criticize Joyce Kilmer's "Trees" on the
purely formal grounds of mixed metaphor instead of on the basis
of the poem's conceptual silliness. Helping students to become
critics is about as difficult as teaching them to become poets,
because both of these functions—criticism and poetry—require
the individual subject to understand his or her place in the world
and to speak *for others*, in a collective voice. I am not trying to
confound poetry and criticism, here, as some theoreticians have
been doing recently, for I believe that directness and clarity are
the principal virtues of criticism and that indirection and subtlety
are among the great strengths of poetry, but we can still recognize that both criticism and poetry require a greater exposure of
the writer's ego, a higher degree of responsibility for what is said
or revealed, than do interpretation and commentary, in which
the ultimate responsibility for meaning is attributed to some
primary text. Both criticism and poetry require more textual
power than reading and interpretation, for they involve extending the domain of textuality further into the untextualized world
while struggling against that which has been textualized already.

I am admitting or conceding, here, the difficulty of teaching
students to be critics, to resist the very texts from which they
derive textual pleasure: to analyze, to dissect, and to oppose.
Of course this is difficult. It is the great aim or end of liberal
education and therefore not something we can assume to be
already developed in students just beginning their college education. But we must start working on the development of critical
skill in our introductory courses. I propose, now, to concentrate
on the kind of analysis that leads to criticism, using the six
bullfighting Interchapters of *In Our Time* as exemplary texts. I
began this section by remarking that no curricular choice is

innocent. My selection of these six bits of text will serve as an example—perhaps a controversial one—of curricular responsibility.

Hemingway himself never put all six of these texts together as a separate unit. In the little *in our time* volume of 1924 the first of them appeared as the second vignette and the others were in sequence as the twelfth through sixteenth. In the larger *In Our Time* of 1925 all six are in sequence as Interchapters nine through fourteen, but they are separated by the larger stories now positioned between them. Putting them together as a unit, then, is something Hemingway himself never quite did, though their sequence within the unit is the same as their sequence on all their other appearances. These are *all* the bullfighting texts from *In Our Time*, and they are in Hemingway's order, but they have been taken out of their final context by me, for instructional purposes. I will ask you, as I have asked my students, to regard them as a single, six-part text, the work of Ernest Hemingway, to see what analytical results we may obtain by this gesture.

One result is that the notion of Hemingway's intention here is made a bit more problematical than usual, but I take that as a pedagogical gain. We can never totally separate an author's intentions from our own. In this case, we have put that little problem out in front. We will then proceed to ignore it—as we *always* ignore it—but with the responsibility for doing so acknowledged from the outset.

Once again, I must ask you to read the texts before trying to follow my discussion of them; and, for the last time, I apologize for not being able to secure the rights to reprint them in full. From this point on, I will refer to the texts by their numerical order in the sequence under discussion, rather than by the Interchapter numbers. These numbers, with the first sentence of the respective text, are given here:

(1) The first matador got the horn through his sword hand and the crowd hooted him.

(2) They whack-whacked the white horse on the legs and he kneed himself up.

(3) The crowd shouted all the time and threw pieces of bread down into the ring, then cushions and leather wine bottles, keeping up whistling and yelling.

(4) If it happened right down close in front of you, you could see Villalta snort at the bull and curse him, and when the bull charged he swung back and forth firmly like an oak when the wind hits it, his legs tight together, the muleta trailing and the sword following the curve behind.

(5) I heard the drums coming down the street and then the fifes and the pipes and then they came around the corner, all dancing.

(6) Maera lay still, his head on his arms, his face in the sand.

In approaching the criticism of this text I would begin by asking students to look for sequential elements that organize and link the six sections. (I am omitting discussion of how each section might be studied in itself, since we have already considered two such examples.) Given the fact that we have six little texts on the same topic, what more specific connections can we find? In discussion I would insist that we begin with the most obvious connections and progressions. For instance, the same proper name, "Maera," appears in (5) and (6). If we assume that both Maeras are the same person or character (a point that would merit some discussion in itself), then we would have to position (5) before (6) in story sequence ("diegetic" time) as well as in reading sequence, since Maera dies in (6). This raises the question of whether the events in (5) are the *cause* of the events in (6). A discussion of this matter will illustrate the importance of what Eco calls the "role of the reader" in narrative construction. Does the frivolous play of Luis *cause* the death of Maera? You decide.

Another obvious connection is the presence of what Hemingway later called "death in the afternoon" in all six sections. Animals die or are dying in four of them; men are wounded or die in two; and the one segment that avoids death, the fifth, ends with a little monologue on killing that is a parody of Molly Bloom's monologue on loving: "we kill them. We kill them all right. Yes. Yes. Yes." The last sentence of the sixth and last segment is "Then he was dead." This is narrative closure with a vengeance. Reading through the whole sequence, students should be able to pick out recurring themes organized as binary oppositions: cowardice and courage; grace and clumsiness; success and failure; life and death. With a little assistance they should also be able to detect more subtle features of narrative structure. There is for instance a progression from youth and inexperience in the first section, through mature perfection in the fourth, to declining powers, pessimism, and finally death in the last two sections. When in the fifth section Luis says, "You're not my father," he positions the narrator and Maera for us in terms of age. Maera's own concluding speech in (5) reveals his pessimism and hints at the fear behind it.

This sequence has a rising and falling structure, then, from the tired, clumsy "kid" killing five bulls, up to the perfect kill executed by Villalta, and down to the *cogida* (getting "hooked" by the bull) and death of Maera. The perfect kill is the high point of the sequence, as the proper name of the *matador* (literally, the "*killer*") indicates: "Villalta" is a combination of two words, *villa*—meaning town, or government of a town, or country seat, residence of power—and *alta*, from the adjective *alto*—meaning high, arduous, eminent—but with an allusion, perhaps, to the noun *alta*, which can refer to a courtly dance, a fencing match, or a clean bill of health. Grace, mystery, eminence—all these are packed into the name Villalta and these connotations are woven through the text that describes his perfect kill:

When he started to kill it was all in the same rush. The bull looking at him straight in front, hating. He drew out the sword from the folds of the muleta and sighted with the same movement and called to the bull, Toro! Toro! and the bull charged and just for a moment they became one. Villalta became one with the bull and then it was over. Villalta standing straight and the red hilt of the sword sticking out dully between the bull's shoulders. Villalta, his hand up at the crowd and the bull roaring blood, looking straight at Villalta and his legs caving.

This exalted moment is presented to us in terms of a little miracle of consubstantiation, in which killer and killed become, "just for a moment," one flesh: "they became one. Villalta became one with the bull and then it was over." In the text, they become one twice: "Became one . . . became one." The moment is held before us by repetition, as in a frozen film image. The name Villalta is repeated also, five times in this paragraph, like an incantation, until it becomes a metonymy for the grace, power, and confidence of the man, and for the sacred moment when the difference between man and beast, life and death, is transcended by a ritual of art and courage. What we must remember, to counteract this incantatory spell, is that we are dealing here with a ritual of language—a composition of words that make a textual unity—as the words *villa* and *alta* do in the matador's name—rather than a fusion of substance.

In the perfect kill, the matador and the bull are atoned: they become one. But the matador lives and the bull dies. The final image in (4) is an exquisite visual composition, worthy of Goya. Villalta with his hand raised, the bull with his legs caving; Villalta's hand, the bull's legs; Villalta up, toward the crowd and the sky, the bull down toward the earth, roaring blood. This much is obvious. What is less obvious but more important for criticism is the way Hemingway has established a complex ratio among three terms in this text:

matador : bull = writer : matador

The matador is to the bull as the writer is to the matador. This will take a bit of explanation.

In teaching this dimension of the text, I would begin by asking students to describe or characterize the narrative voice or presence that we encounter in each of the six sections. The result of the ensuing discussion should be something like this. In (1) the narrator is inexperienced, perhaps a "kid" himself. There is no special terminology in this segment; on the contrary, a sentence like "He couldn't hardly lift his arm" has echoes of the boyish tones of Huck Finn or Sherwood Anderson's "Fool." Close examination of other phrases will confirm this. The voice in (2), on the other hand, is much less excited and more knowledgeable. This voice uses terms like "picadors" and "monos" (*monosabios*, red-bloused bullring servants) that connote the speaker's familiarity with the code of bullfighting. It is, in fact, more of a "voice" and less of a "person" than the narrative presence of the first segment. It is very calm, remote, speaking of "entrails" where the first narrator would have spoken of "guts." This narrator is a detached, invisible presence, calmly noting the color and movement of the hanging entrails and closing down the narrative at a moment of indecision. This is a camera-eye or slice-of-life style.

The narrator of (3) is even more knowledgeable, but perhaps the knowledge is so recent that he feels obliged to display it in terms like *cuadrilla* and *puntillo* ("crew" and "dagger"). He describes more sharply and with more detail than the narrator of (1). The crowd in (1) is described as hooting and hollering— cliché words (hootin' and hollerin') that tell us more about the narrator than about the crowd—while in (3) the crowd "shouted all the time . . . keeping up yelling and whistling." In (1) the crowd throws "things," while in (3) the crowd throws "pieces of bread . . . then cushions and leather wine bottles." I am not trying to make a value judgment here, only to show how in (1) the center of interest is on the narrator himself and his impressions, while (3) gives us more of the scene. The narrator of (1) seems new to bullfighting, an outsider, too impressed and excited to be precise about anything. In (2) we get detachment and precision. In (3) we encounter a narrator who can be precise but who is also a character in the world he is describing. Here we meet the pronoun "I" for the first time in this sequence. The narrator is not only a spectator at the bullfight he describes; he is also a person who can engage the bullfighter in conversation at a café after the fight. He is *in* the world of bullfighting and can give the reader inside information, the very words of the incompetent matador. We get different narrators and different matadors in each segment of this text, but in a larger sense the writer is closing in on the matador as the matador closes with the bull. They will "become one" at the kill.

In (4) we are given a striking use of second-person narration, bringing the reader directly into the scene, allowing us to have the impression that everything is happening before our eyes: "If it happened right down close in front of you, you could see. . . ." It *does* happen right down close in front of us in this segment, and the prose rhythms and audio-visual detail construct a powerful illusion. Are we the matador or the bull in this little drama? Or are we safely behind the barrera? I think the reader is both the bull and the crowd in this scene. Both are being "played" by the great Villalta, whose movements with the muleta cause the bull to charge and the crowd to roar: "Then he cursed the bull, flopped down the muleta at him, and swung back from the charge his feet firm, the muleta curving and at each swing the crowd roaring." The syntactic structure here links the muleta and the crowd by parallel constructions: "the muleta curving . . . the crowd roaring." Villalta controls both with his movements, just as he controls the bull's movements. Both the bull and the crowd are described in the same word: "roaring." We have seen how many words Hemingway uses for crowd noise: "hooted," "hollered," "shouted," "whistling and yelling." But in (4) the only word is "roaring," the very word used for the bull's last gasp. In the last sentence we are shown Villalta with his "hand up at the crowd" and "the bull roaring blood." The construction and punctuation of this sentence, however, are such that we are offered another grouping of these words: "the crowd and the bull roaring." The crowd has already been described as "roaring" in this segment, and we assume it is roaring still, as the bull roars out his bloody death and Villalta lifts his undoubtedly bloody hand. When Hemingway lifts his hand from the page, Villalta and the crowd will be as dead as the bull. Are we cheering him? Are we roaring? Are we roaring blood?

In (5) the narrator *is* a matador. He is no longer a spectator, even one who talks to matadors in cafés. He is himself an actor in the events narrated. But he is not yet holding the muleta or killing a bull. It is the morning before the *corrida* ("you've got bulls this afternoon") in which the narrator will kill at last. He is an old hand here, who treats Luis like a kid ("I grabbed his arm") and is told off as a kid rejects a father ("oh leave me alone"), though he is not a father ("You're not my father"). The relationship between the narrator and Luis (the "ignorant Mexican savage") is a version of the relationship between the narrator and the Magyar in "The Revolutionist." Mature, responsible man tries to get happy-go-lucky boy to face stern realities. Boy goes his own way. Trouble follows. Obviously, imagining things this way brought pleasure and satisfaction to the young Hemingway. He enjoyed putting himself in the role of a seasoned veteran in a dangerous trade. This, too, is a kind of textual pleasure and a function of textual power.

In the sixth section all the narrators are gone. We are inside Maera, sharing his last moments, except for an occasional piece of outside information, such as where the doctor had been before coming to attend Maera (in the corral, "sewing up picador horses"). We are not only inside Maera, we are inside bullfighting, backstage, under the grandstand, where we can hear a "great shouting" but will never know what it was about. For the first time, in this sequence, we share sensations that are not spectatorial: "Once the horn went all the way through him and he felt it go into the sand." The last sentences of the text report the final sensations of a failing nervous system. The controlling metaphor for this is a motion picture projector that has lost its synchronicity with the human perceptive mechanism. Maera dies as a spectator of his own death: "Then everything commenced to run faster and faster as when they speed up a cinematograph film. Then he was dead." The reel is empty, the screen has gone white; no more images, no more spectating, no more life. The narrator has become the matador but the matador is dying instead of killing, and in dying he becomes a spectator. The crowd is shouting, but he will never know for whom the crowd shouts—nor will we. After the word "dead" we face blank white paper ourselves. The technical proficiency of this work is of the highest order. Formally, it is very close to perfection. How, then, can we criticize it?

If (6) takes place on the afternoon of (5)—a narrative connection the reader is invited to make—and if events have gone as Maera predicted, then Luis has been wounded and Maera has got a fatal *cogida*. This leaves only one matador, as we learned in segment (1), to kill the remaining bulls. And this matador must be the narrator of (5), whom we know only as "I." In the figure of "I," who is being cheered as Maera dies, we encounter Hemingway's projection of himself into the narrative. While we, the readers, are down below the grandstand, dying with Maera, the author is offstage but on stage—not, like Joyce's artist-god, paring his fingernails, but, like Villalta, killing and being cheered for it by the gratified spectators. The author is also with us, of course, chronicling Maera's last picture show.

As the matador kills the bull and becomes one with the bull in the aesthetic ritual of the *corrida*, the writer kills the matador and becomes one with the matador in the aesthetic ritual that is Hemingway's text. There can be no question that Hemingway dispatches Maera with a grace and beauty equivalent to that of Villalta as he kills his last bull and raises his triumphant hand to the crowd. For criticism to do more than emit a bloody roar and collapse in admiration here, the critic must, as Eco suggests in the epigraph to this chapter, adopt an ideological bias that will make Hemingway's text "say more than it apparently says," in order "to find out what in that text is ideologically presupposed, untold." The critical project we are embarked upon here consists of finding a stance sufficiently antagonistic to Hemingway's to bring his "untold" presuppositions to light. The act of freeing ourselves from the power of his text depends upon our finding a position outside the assumptions upon which the text is based.

Since the text is clearly based upon a pervasive aestheticizing of its world, our antagonistic position must challenge the position of literary art itself.

Hemingway is firmly entrenched in modernist values in this text. He has taken what for many is a repulsive, anachronistic slaughter and turned it into a sequence of exquisite vignettes. Even the "blue bunch" of the white horse's entrails is included and forced by the textual power of Hemingway's prose into an aesthetic image that might easily be rewritten in the manner of a modernist poem:

> so much depends
> upon
>
> the blue bunch of
> entrails
>
> swinging backward and
> forward
>
> beneath the white
> horse.

The William Carlos Williams poem from which I have borrowed a syntax here was in fact written at the same time (1923) as the Hemingway sketches. This was the moment of the objective correlative, the moment when literature was most firmly rejecting the contingent and historical, striving for the permanent, the mythic, the concrete universal of art. Hemingway, very much a part of that movement, was trying to cross a gap he had defined as the difference between timely journalism and timeless art:

> In writing for a newspaper you told what happened and, with one trick and another, you communicated the emotion aided by the element of timeliness which gives a certain emotion to any account of something that has happened on that day; but the real thing, the sequence of motion and fact which made the emotion and which would be as valid in a year or in ten years or, with luck and if you stated it purely enough, always, was beyond me and I was working very hard to get it. The only place

where you could see life and death, *i.e.* violent death now that
the wars were over, was in the bull ring and I wanted very much
to go to Spain where I could study it. I was trying to learn to
write, commencing with the simplest things, and one of the
simplest things of all and the most fundamental is violent death.
[*Death in the Afternoon*, p. 2][1]

What Hemingway found in the bullring was, as he tells us,
too much for his "then equipment for writing to deal with." He
wanted to make the things before him "permanent, as, say,
Goya tried to make them in *Los Desastros de la Guerra.*" But,
where Goya's paintings and sketches of the Napoleonic wars had
a powerful ethical and political dimension, Hemingway found in
bullfighting an absolute divorce between the political and the
ethical. The spectators, he said, "pay to see the tragedy of the
bull" (*DIA*, p. 162), but the animal has no tragedy unless we
project upon it a human intelligence. The spectacle that Hemingway came to admire was in fact the last true survivor of
ancient Roman bread and circuses, a ritual that seemed natural
for those raised within its cultural circle, but would always
remain exotic for those brought up in more modern Western
cultures. Caught up in Hemingway's search for the "pure" style
that would capture an emotion "permanently" was a civilized
nostalgia for a barbaric world of tragedy and triumph. This truly
and deeply reactionary level of thought is always present in
Hemingway's most progressive or socially conscious moments.
To capture the *emotion* of socialism is the goal of the passage on
art and politics from *For Whom the Bell Tolls* (quoted above in
chapter 3, p. 46).

The only way to gain a measure of critical freedom from the
emotionally powerful text of these bullfight sketches is to bring
reason to bear upon the emotion and to question the aestheticizing of death itself. It was Goya, of course, who reminded us that
the sleep of reason produces monsters, and history continues to
substantiate his case. In seeing the beauty of the corrida—and
sometimes the beauty of war itself ("It was absolutely topping.

They tried to get over it and we potted them from forty yards"
—Interchapter IV.)—Hemingway is not simply wrong. He is
getting at a truth that we would rather forget: that men love
certain aspects of violent, fatal combat. But his frequent en-
dorsement of that view, his own love affair with violence and
death, should allow us to position ourselves critically: with him
or against him—or both—by choice. And that is the whole
function of criticism. It is a way of discovering how to choose,
how to take some measure of responsibility for ourselves and for
our world. Criticism is our last best chance to loosen the bonds of
the textual powers in which we find ourselves enmeshed.

5

THE TEXT AND THE WORLD

"Textuality" is the somewhat mystical
and disinfected subject matter of literary theory. . . . As it is practiced in
the American academy today, literary
theory has for the most part isolated
textuality from the circumstances, the
events, the physical senses that made it
possible and render it intelligible as the
result of human work.

Edward Said,
The World, the Text, and the Critic

The accusation brought against literary theory by Edward Said
in the epigraph is of the utmost gravity. Contemporary theory
has given us, he charges, an impoverished notion of textuality, in
which the literary text is perceived as forever cut off from reality
by its very literariness, its special kind of textuality. It is not
clear, in Said's formulation, whether he believes that this is the
inevitable condition of literary theory or the result of theory's
imprisonment in a particular cultural situation. At times Said
seems to suggest that a theoretician like Fredric Jameson or
Michel Foucault might be able to transcend the isolationism of
theory, but when he looks carefully into a particular case, as he
does with Foucault, he finds this critic ultimately taking "a
curiously passive and sterile view" of the pragmatics of textual
power (*WTC*, p. 221). For Said, theory is not fruitful unless it
culminates in criticism. As he says of Foucault, but surely means
to proclaim as a general principle,

Where there is knowledge and discourse, there must criticism also be, to reveal the exact places—and displacements—of the text, thereby to see the text as a process signifying an effective historical will to be present, an effective desire to be a text and to be a position taken. [*WTC*, p. 221.]

It is in fact this will to textual power that makes the opening for criticism. But whether the critic can enter that opening will depend entirely upon his or her theory of textuality.

At times Said seems to suggest that to become a critic one must explicitly renounce theory, because contemporary literary theory has "turned its back on" the world, to embrace "the aporias and unthinkable paradoxes of a text." Said argues that the critic must explicitly reject the "priestly caste of acolytes and dogmatic metaphysicians" (*WTC*, pp. 4, 5). Though I might not put it in precisely those terms, I am in sympathy with Said's view of this matter. In the earlier chapters of this book I have repeatedly tried to make explicit certain connections between texts and the world. But in doing so I have not really faced the question of a theoretical justification for this practice. The question, however, must be faced, not only in books like this but in our classrooms as well. The relationship between a text and the world is not a given but a problem. (Even in writing the previous sentence I hesitated among *the* world, *a* world, *its* world, and *our* world. My choice, naturally, supports my own position. Whole philosophies may come to stand on a single article or pronoun, like angels on the head of a pin.)

The relationship between text and world is not simply a fascinating problem for textual theory. It is, above all others, the problem that makes textual theory necessary. At the present time there are two major positions that can be taken with respect to this problem, and, as we shall see in the case of Fredric Jameson, it is extremely difficult to combine them or find any middle ground between them. Following Said's distinction between the Batinist and Zahirite interpreters of the Koran, we may call these two positions *secular* and *hermetic* (not hermeneutic, please note, but hermetic). The secular or worldly critics see texts as historically grounded in public occasions and socially supported codes. The hermetic interpreters see texts as radically self-reflective and non-referential—and therefore beyond the reach of criticism. These two positions are clearly exemplified in the recent work of Terry Eagleton and Paul de Man, the most pointed contrast occurring in their definitions of rhetoric.

In his spirited romp through the past few decades of studies in the theory of literature,[1] Eagleton argues consistently for a radical restructuring of literary study into a broader investigation of discursive practices of all sorts, which he proposes to call rhetoric. This revival of an old discipline would take as its object the *use* of texts of all sorts in all media, holding as its major critical principle the view that all texts are grounded in ideology. Such a rhetoric would cover "both the practice of effective discourse and the science of it": that is, the modes of production, the media of presentation, and the effects of reception. And it would consider "the various sign systems and signifying practices in our own society, all the way from *Moby Dick* to the Muppet show, from Dryden and Jean-Luc Goddard to the portrayal of women in advertisements and the rhetorical techniques of Government reports" (*Literary Theory*, p. 207).

Eagleton's program is clear enough. It is, in fact, very much like the Program in Semiotic Studies that has been in operation at Brown University for the past decade. But his theoretical justification of that program is not always adequate to its occasion. He suggests, for instance, that we "draw the practical consequences of the fact that literary theory can handle Bob Dylan just as well as John Milton" (*LT*, p. 205). By "practical consequences" he seems to mean that the ability of theory to "handle" the work of these two men equally well means that the work itself is in some sense equivalent. But surely any theory that prevented us from distinguishing between Milton's work and Dylan's would raise serious questions about its own adequacy. It is important, for instance, to bring poetry, painting, and advertising into the same frame of reference, in order to discover their shared repertory of techniques and to expose whatever ideological complicity exists among them, as John Berger has done, for instance, in *Ways of Seeing*, his illuminating study of the connection between oil painting and advertising images,[2] but it is also important to recognize the differences in the modes of production, media of expression, methods of distribution, and the uses of these different kinds of text. The egalitarian impulse, which is such a powerful motive in Eagleton's argument, may itself threaten criticism by preventing it from seeing differences where they must be seen in order for us to act upon them. I accept the principle that criticism must be ideologically based. That was, in fact, a theme of the preceding chapter. But I insist—and will argue the case in chapter 9—that our critical position does not totally control our perception of texts. Any excess in Eagleton's position, however, is more than balanced by excesses on the other side, where we encounter arguments that begin by granting the special status of literature only to texts that are innocent of contamination by reference to the world and conclude by claiming that all texts are literary in that both communication and reference are beyond them.

What is at stake in the struggle between secular and hermetic theories of textuality can be brought into focus by comparing Eagleton's notion of rhetoric to that proposed by Paul de Man. Except for its extension beyond the verbal to include all semiotic processes, Eagleton's view is quite traditional. He sees rhetoric as the study of how texts are used to perform work in the world. Examining the traditional distinction between *rhetoric* and *poetry*, the text that *means* and the text that *is*, the text for *persuasion* and the text for *contemplation*, Eagleton assumes that this binary opposition is false, since all texts have their meanings and persuasive ends. All are rhetorical. Examining this same traditional distinction in Part I of *Allegories of Reading*,[3] de Man also insists that all texts are rhetorical, but what he means by rhetoric is what has traditionally been meant by poetry. For de Man, everything that is a text is rhetorical, and rhetoric itself is a text. This will require some explanation.

De Man introduces the question of rhetoric by examining a rhetorical question drawn from what he calls "the subliterature of the mass media."

> Asked by his wife whether he wants to have his bowling shoes laced over or laced under, Archie Bunker answers with a question: "What's the difference?" Being a reader of sublime simplicity, his wife replies by patiently explaining the difference between lacing over and lacing under, whatever this may be, but provokes only ire. "What's the difference" did not ask for difference but means instead "I don't give a damn what the difference is." The same grammatical pattern engenders two meanings that are mutually exclusive: the literal meaning asks for the concept (difference) whose existence is denied by the figurative meaning. [*AR*, p. 9]

Considering this text and other instances of rhetorical questions, de Man concludes that "the grammatical model of the question becomes rhetorical not when we have, on the one hand, a literal meaning and on the other hand a figurative meaning but when it is impossible to decide . . . which of two meanings . . . prevails (*AR*, p. 10). Rhetoric, as the hesitation between literal and figurative meanings, becomes for de Man that discourse which cannot be deconstructed because it refuses to assert, persuade, or refer unequivocally. It is itself already "the deconstructive discourse that we call literary, or rhetorical, or poetic" (*AR*, p. 18). "Rhetoric is a *text* in that it allows for two incompatible, mutually self-destructive points of view, and therefore puts an insurmountable obstacle in the way of any reading or understanding" (*AR*, p. 131).

Where Eagleton sought to bring all texts under the rubric of rhetoric, de Man seeks to bring them all under the rubric of literature, which he chooses to call "rhetoric." Thus, de Man's act of appropriation is far more drastic than Eagleton's. For de Man, if there are texts that allow themselves to be read univocally, thus submitting to "understanding," they are neither rhetorical nor poetic. They are, in fact, only collections of words, not texts at all. He makes an effort, of course, to weave his own words into a text that is properly rhetorical—impervious to any reading or understanding—because he believes that the difference between criticism and literature is "delusive." For de Man, textual power is a function of the text's resistance to reading. The strength of this position derives from its being a version of our deeply held conviction that the "best" texts are those that require interpretation. But there is a twist—another turn of the screw—in de Man's version of this position. For him, the function of interpretation is to show how every text requires interpretation. This screw turns endlessly without ever fastening one thing to another. Taking the New Critical privileging of irony and paradox to the very edge of absurdity, de Man's theory of textuality denies the possibility of "fastening." What makes a text a text is the impossibility of connecting it to the world.

Said challenges this view, but he is too respectful of de Man to confront him as its principal exemplar. Eagleton is well aware of the relationship between his position and that of de Man and the "Yale School." In two corrosive pages he reaches the accurate conclusion that for this group, "Literature is the ruin of all reference, the cemetery of communication." As he describes this position, the hermetic theoreticians have not been content with showing that literature is "unreadable," they have "colonized" history itself, viewing "famines, revolutions, soccer matches, and sherry trifle as yet more undecidable 'text' " (*LT*, p. 146). Eagleton's position is plain enough. If the world is a text and texts are undecidable, then "prudent men and women" will have a perfect excuse for inaction on social questions. De Man's position can be condemned on the grounds that it results in a quietistic acceptance of injustice. To condemn it thus, however, one must assume the opposite view: that the world is really knowable, either because it is not a text or because texts are finally intelligible after all. This seems to me a perfectly proper assumption, but it must also be argued as a case, because it is now a major area of contention in the field of textual studies. As I suggested earlier, the middle ground between the secular and hermetic positions is a treacherous no-man's-land, as we shall learn from observing Fredric Jameson's attempt to occupy it in *The Political Unconscious*.

Jameson's awareness of the need to occupy this difficult terrain is apparent upon every page of his book but nowhere more so than in his attempt to mitigate the Althusserian critique of historical causality:

> The sweeping negativity of the Althusserian formula is misleading insofar as it can readily be assimilated to the polemic themes of a host of contemporary post-structuralisms and post-Marxisms, for which History, in the bad sense—the reference to a "context" or a "ground," an external real world of some kind, the reference, in other words, to the much maligned "referent" itself—is simply one more text among others. . . . but . . . he does not at all draw the fashionable conclusion that because history is a text, the "referent" does not exist. We would therefore propose the following revised formulation: that history is *not* a text . . . but that . . . it is inaccessible to us except in textual form. [*PU*, p. 35]

Jameson is clearly looking for a middle ground here, between the secular position (which is that of traditional Marxists, among others) and the hermetic position of the "post-structuralisms and post-Marxisms." He has some kind words to say for the "much maligned 'referent'," but he keeps the creature handcuffed with quotation marks. His mediating formula is that "history is not a text . . . but that . . . it is inaccessible to us except in textual form." This is an elegant formulation, but it does not really address the problem posed by the post-structuralist theory of textuality. The problem is not really a matter of the referent but of reference; it is not a question of whether the world exists but of whether we can perceive it or refer to it adequately.

Accepting the reality of the world (or postulating it, if you prefer) does not really solve the problem of how we know anything about it or whether we can speak or write about it. As we have seen, de Man and the hermetic theoreticians have raised

Prob & Relevance

the epistemological ante by claiming that the problem of reference is exacerbated by the problem of sense. In the hermetic
formulation, texts are not only non-referential, they are unintel-
ligible as well, putting insurmountable obstacles "in the way of
any reading or understanding" (*AR*, p. 131). But for Jameson
texts are not only intelligible, they can be made to yield up their
subtexts as well:

> The type of interpretation here proposed is more satisfactorily
> grasped as a rewriting of the literary text in such a way that the
> latter may itself be seen as the rewriting or restructuration of a
> prior historical or ideological *subtext*, it being always under-
> stood that that subtext is not immediately present as such, not
> some common-sense external reality, nor even the conven-
> tional narratives of the history manuals, but rather must itself
> always be (re)constructed after the fact. [*PU*, p. 81, italics in
> original]

The question this formulation raises is *how* we discover the
subtext in the literary text. If, as Jameson observes frequently in
this book, all interpretation is allegorical, we can locate the
historical (which we must do in order to perceive the ideological
as ideological) only by referring the text to some interpretive
code already in place for us, some *view* of history. We cannot
simply find the historical in the text. Put simply, we must have a
way of distinguishing those elements in a text that are the fantastic offspring of the political unconscious, and those other elements that are signs of the reality which this unconscious is trying
to repress. We cannot arrive at the referent without a road map.
Without a notion of the real we cannot even hope to recognize
fantasy as fantasy. To accomplish what he wants to accomplish,
Jameson must insist that the Marxist narrative of history is *not* a
narrative, *not a text*, but he is too deeply implicated in hermetic
thought to assert this. Therefore he leaves vague or blurred the
whole matter of reference.

One of the most revealing passages in *The Political Unconscious*, with respect to Jameson's failure to deal with the problem of reference, is his discussion of *mediation* as an interpretive

device. By *mediation* Jameson means the textual conjunction of actual things,

> . . . the invention of an analytic terminology or code which can be applied equally to two or more structurally distinct objects or sectors of being. As we [earlier] argued, it is not necessary that these analyses be homologous, that is, that each of the objects in question be seen as doing the same thing, having the same structure or emitting the same message. What is crucial is that, by being able to use the same language about each of these quite distinct objects or levels of an object, we can restore, at least methodologically, the lost unity of social life, and demonstrate that widely distant elements of the social totality are ultimately part of the same global historical process. [*PU*, pp. 225–26]

By connecting different "objects or sectors of being" (a euphemism for real things) in the "same language," Jameson claims to be able to restore ("at least methodologically") "the lost unity of social life." This is textual power with a vengeance. Let us consider more closely some of the implications of this passage:

(1) The application of "an analytic terminology or code" can achieve the textualization of an "object" or "sector of being." In short, with the right code, reference is no problem.

(2) The taking up of two or more objects in the same discourse constitutes a link between the objects not only in the text but in the world outside the text. Not only is reference achieved by the right "analytic terminology," but so is power over the objects referred to. They are connected by the text.

(3) Such textual connections not only link the named objects but "restore . . . the lost unity of social life." The waste land of reification is cured by utterance of the analytic terminology.

(4) This restoration of lost unity may only be methodological—or textual—after all, which leads to' the conclusion, developed at some length in Jameson's last chapter, that if the actual always confounds the textual, the solution is to live inside textuality, where lost unities can really be restored.

Despite certain excerptable calls to arms of the secular party, especially apparent as the first and last words of the book

("Always historicize!" and "political praxis . . . remains . . .
what Marxism is all about") this text is finally as undecidable as
any hermetic critic could wish it to be. This fundamental hermeticism is nowhere more apparent than in those passages in which
Jameson offers a direct textual linkage between two "sectors of
being." Consider the following quotations, in which the "same
language" of connection is employed. (My italics.)

> Marxist critical insights will therefore here be defended as
> *something like* an ultimate semantic precondition. . . . [*PU*, p.
> 75]
>   . . . making the "hero" over into *something like* a register-
> ing apparatus. . . . [p. 112]
>   . . . we have sometimes seemed to begin . . . with a strong
> term . . . of which the later versions are . . . *something like* a
> dissolution. . . . [p. 139]
>   The fantasy level of a text would then be *something like* the
> primal motor force. . . . [p. 142]
>   Yet the point . . . is not simply to establish *something like*
> Plekhanov's "social equivalent" . . . . [p. 148]
>   . . . the possibility of *something like* a system of characters
> remains unexplored. . . . [p. 162]
>   Our reading . . . is thus *something like* a lateral by-product
> of our initial attention. . . . [p. 163]
>   The latter is thus . . . *something like* a bystander. . . . [p.
> 174]
>   . . . human sexuality is *something like* a fixed capital. . . .
> [p. 178]
>   Gissing thus finds himself limited to *something like* an
> indicative mode. . . . [p. 196]
>   . . . the novel comes to be considered as *something like* a
> laboratory space. . . . [p. 197]
>   . . . its constituent features . . . suggest *something like* a
> rigorous and depersonalized use. . . . [p. 203]
>   The dialectic of desire is thus in Gissing *something like* the
> negation of a negation. . . . [p. 205]
>   . . . which may thus be read as *something like* the final
> form. . . . [p. 205]
>   . . . will serve as *something like* a pretext. . . . [p. 209]

In the quoted passages an equivocal device that all writers
fall back upon occasionally is used so extensively that it becomes
the dominant principle of discourse. The expression "something
like" is not only the weakest possible form of comparison, it
logically implicates its own contradiction (something *un*like)
and thus attains the same nonsensical status as the de Manic
rhetorical question. It becomes radically unreadable, beyond
sense as well as beyond reference. Jameson's text, which is full
of serious thought and learning, is also astonishingly reluctant
to emerge from its own web of textuality to make contact with
the world. It is in this context that we should view Jameson's
claims on behalf of what he calls the "structuralist or textual
revolution," an anti-empiricist mode of thought that

> drives the wedge of the concept of a "text" into the traditional
> disciplines by extrapolating the notion of "discourse" or "writ-
> ing" onto objects previously thought to be "realities" or objects
> in the real world, such as the various levels or instances of a
> social formation: political power, social class, institutions, and
> events themselves. When properly used, the concept of the
> "text" does not, as in garden-variety semiotic practice today,
> "reduce" these realities to small and manageable written doc-
> uments of one kind or another, but rather liberates us from the
> empirical object—whether institution, event, or individual
> work—by displacing our attention to its *constitution* as an ob-
> ject and its *relationship* to the other objects thus constituted.
> [*PU*, pp. 296–97, italics in original]

Jameson argues here that the "textual revolution," in which
he clearly considers himself a participant, has freed us from the
"empirical object" and given us textual objects in its place. By
textual objects I assume he means the sort of institutions studied
by Michel Foucault in *Discipline and Punish*,[4] for instance, or
even the English apparatus we considered briefly in the first
chapter of this book, that is to say, real objects that function like
texts because they are cultural. But even studies like Foucault's,
of cultural objects, depend upon a grounding in empirical objects: dates, documents, buildings, practices, and so on, as a

glance at Foucault's notes will reveal. Seeing institutions as discursive creatures, caught up in webs of textuality even while spinning new ones, does *not* free us from "the empirical object," which, I fear, is simply the "much maligned 'referent'" in another textual disguise. The real threat to a new secular textuality is not some "garden variety semiotic practice" that reduces "realities" to "small and manageable written documents," it is a rampant, de Manic hermeticism that supplants realities with the undecidable toils of its own form of textuality.

If Jameson's attempt to link the secular and the hermetic fails, as I think it does despite its intellectual richness and thoughtfulness, it is because one cannot rescue the much maligned referent while remaining liberated from the empirical object. The only path that may lead us toward a new secular theory of textuality begins by leading us backward. We shall have to make some attempt to rescue the referent, to rehabilitate reference itself, before moving on to a new textual practice—and we must do this without falling back into naive assumptions about the empirical object. This task will not be easy for the writer, the reader, or the text.

6

REFERENCE AND DIFFERENCE

Philosophers and bookish people generally tend to live a life dominated by words, and even to forget that it is the essential function of words to have a connection of some sort or another with facts, which are in general non-linguistic. Some modern philosophers have gone so far as to say that words should never be confronted with facts but should live in a pure, autonomous world where they are compared only with other words. When you say, "the cat is a carnivorous animal," you do not mean that actual cats eat actual meat, but only that in zoology books the cat is classified among carnivora. These authors tell us that the attempt to confront language with fact is "metaphysics" and is on this ground to be condemned. This is one of those views which are so absurd that only very learned men could possibly adopt them.

Bertrand Russell,
My Philosophical Development

As the epigraph from Russell indicates, the attack on reference is not an invention of post-structuralist theory; nevertheless, it is an important element in the post-structuralist position, where it functions as a major support for the hermetic view of textuality. This chapter is my attempt to blunt the attack on reference by a counterattack on the notion of "difference," as it has been developed in the post-structuralist theory of language and texts.

In particular, I want to challenge the notion that language is a system of "pure differences," for it is this notion upon which the attack on reference is presently based. I will not deny that language is based on difference; rather, I will argue that it is also based upon reference, a dimension of the human use of language that has been systematically repressed or ignored by structuralist and hermetic theoreticians.

The position I have been calling "hermetic" is also sometimes called "deconstructive." This can be confusing because, as I will show in the chapter after this one, certain features of deconstruction can be used for secular ends—indeed I made use of them in that way in chapter 1. But in this chapter I will use the term "deconstruction" as it is used by the more hermetic followers of Derrida and de Man. The most accessible statement of this party's views is that presented by Jonathan Culler in *On Deconstruction* and in his monograph *Ferdinand de Saussure*.[1] The theory of language presented in these two books will be the main object of my critique, not because I hold Culler personally responsible for it but because his is the strongest and clearest presentation of this position.

In *On Deconstruction* Culler tells us that Saussure

> concludes that "in the linguistic system there are only differences, *without positive terms*" (*Cours*, p. 166/120). This is a radical formulation. The common view is doubtless that a language consists of words, positive entities, which are put together to form a system and thus acquire relations with one another, but Saussure's analysis of the nature of linguistic units leads to the conclusion that, on the contrary, signs are the product of a system of differences; indeed, they are not positive entities at all but effects of difference. This is a powerful critique of logocentrism. [*OD*, pp. 98–99]

In this passage Culler is adjusting Saussure's view to harmonize with the deconstructive theory of language. To do this he must suppress the fact that on the following page of Saussure's *Course in General Linguistics* he takes the opposite position, saying,

"When we compare signs—positive terms—with each other, we can no longer speak of difference" (*CGL*, p. 121).[2] At the very least, one can say that a splendid opportunity to show Saussure deconstructing himself has been overlooked. I do not want to trivialize Culler's achievement here. He has given us an excellent book on structuralism (*Structuralist Poetics*) and a very good one on semiotics (*The Pursuit of Signs*).[3] The twin strengths of these books are his skill at exposition of complex ideas and his ability to stand outside the ideas he is explaining and oppose to them a critical position of his own. In the books on Saussure and Deconstruction, however, the expositor often triumphs over the critic, smoothing out difficulties that might have been better faced, or erasing from the record traces that should have been acknowledged. In the case of Saussure, however, there is more than this at stake. In dealing with Saussure, one can either attempt to extract from him a coherent view of language, which the texts we have do not really provide, or one can look seriously at the problems and try to sort out the assumptions that need to be reexamined. In my own view, there are massive problems at the very basis of Saussure's theory of language. Culler, in becoming Saussure's expositor, and in positioning Saussure to function as Derrida's precursor, has glossed over or closed down certain problems and pathways that it seems to me essential to open up.

One of the clues to this glossing over is the personification of language itself that Culler resorts to in his discussion of "The Nature of Linguistic Units."

A language does not simply assign arbitrary names to a set of independently existing concepts. It sets up an arbitrary relationship between signifiers of *its own choosing* on the one hand, and signifieds of *its own choosing* on the other. Not only does each language produce a set of signifiers articulating and dividing the continuum of sound in a distinctive way, but each language produces a different set of signifieds; it has a distinctive and thus "arbitrary" way of organizing the world into concepts or categories. [*FS*, p. 15, my italics]

I have emphasized the phrases which attribute an active voli-
tional quality to language, because these personifications are
clues to the problem that Culler is trying to gloss over in this
passage. The problem, as Ferrucio Rossi-Landi indicates in his
fascinating study of the "Whorf-Sapir hypothesis," is "that there
are both different thoughts 'in' the same language, and the same
thought 'in' different languages."[4] But we do not have to look at
Navajo and Hopi to conclude this. Actually, we need look no
farther than Saussure himself.

Saussure argues that the bond between signifier and signified
is arbitrary. Culler and others have made much of the radical
originality of this insight, but it is in fact a commonplace which
Saussure has received from the tradition of John Locke (especially as interpreted by Condillac).[5] Locke himself is completely
unequivocal on the matter. In discussing the question of how
words came to be the signs of ideas (in a vocabulary not so
different from Saussure's terminology of sound-images and concepts or signifiers and signifieds) Locke answers the question as
follows in *An Essay Concerning Human Understanding*: "not
by any natural connexion that there is between particular and
articulate sounds and certain ideas, for then there would be but
one language amongst all men; but by a voluntary imposition,
whereby such a word is made *arbitrarily* the mark of such an
idea" (my italics).[6] Locke's dubious "voluntary" haunts all his
followers down through Culler. But his position can be clearly
distinguished from Saussure's. For Locke it is the signifier or
"word" that is arbitrarily assigned to "ideas" already present in
the mind as the result of "sensations" acquired by the actions of
the senses upon the "white paper, void of all characters" that is
the mind. How is it for Saussure?

Culler tells us that Saussure believed not only in the arbitrariness of the sound-images or signifiers in any language, and in
the arbitrary connection between any particular signifier and
any particular signified; he tells us also that Saussure believed
that "each language produces a different set of signifieds; it has a
distinctive and thus 'arbitrary' way of organizing the world into

concepts and categories" (*FS*, p. 15). The glide from "distinctive" to "arbitrary" here, lubricated by a deft "thus," is deceptively easy. Two things may be different simply because they are motivated in different ways. This formulation also glides over the question of just how different the "set of signifieds" found in different languages may actually be. One of Saussure's first illustrations of arbitrariness brings the problem squarely before us. He points out that "the signified 'ox' has as its signifier b-ö-f on one side of the border" between France and Germany "and o-k-s *(Ochs)* on the other" (*CGL*, p. 68). But this example can in no way convince us that these languages have what Culler calls "a different set of signifieds," since Saussure himself placidly indicates that the *same signified* ("the signified 'ox'") exists in both languages, thus contradicting the notion that every language "chooses its own signifieds." The signifiers may be accidental or random (whatever they are, they are not "chosen") but the signifieds are not. They are to a high degree based upon the perceived presence of oxen upon both sides of the border.

Saussure had indeed demonstrated, like Locke before him, that the link between signifier and signified was arbitrary, but he went on to claim that signifieds or concepts were also arbitrary, which he could not demonstrate. Saussure's contemporary, Charles S. Peirce, the other godfather of modern semiotics, was developing a theory of signs at about the same time as Saussure. He argued that every sign (Saussure's "signifier") must be interpreted by another sign (Peirce's "interpretant"), so that signification is an endless network, linking sign to sign. Derrida has combined Saussure's notion of the arbitrary sign with Peirce's notion of unlimited semiosis—the endless network of signs—in articulating his own theory of the instituted trace. This combination is powerful, especially since Derrida could accomplish what Saussure could not. He could mount an attack on perception itself that apparently cut the ground out from under all theories of meaning that depend upon reference to objects in any way. We shall return to Derrida's critique of reference, but first we must pause to examine more thoroughly Saussure's definition of the sign.

For Saussure the word "sign" meant "verbal sign" most of the time, for it is the verbal sign—as opposed to the visual or iconic sign, for instance—that is marked by an arbitrary signifier. For those influenced by Saussure, the supposed purity or arbitrariness of the verbal sign is a major element of all consideration of signs. Derrida's "traces" are more like Saussurean verbal signs than anything else, as his own illustrations of this concept in phonemic terms (*Positions*, p. 26, for instance) clearly demonstrate.[7] Thus, when Peirce's notion that every sign must be interpreted by another sign is translated into Saussurean terms, it leads to the conclusion that every verbal sign is connected to another verbal sign: crudely, every word is defined by another word, in an endless chain, which is hopelessly cut off from nonverbal affairs. This situation, which Fredric Jameson used to call the "prison house of language" before he found himself inside the walls, is presently based not only upon Saussure's weak claims about the arbitrariness of the sign but also upon Derrida's much more subtle attack upon perception and reference. Derrida's own view, however, is founded upon Saussure's, which is itself in conflict with that of Peirce and many other students of signification. In a late paper, Peirce described his position this way:

(It is important to understand what I mean by *semiosis*. All dynamical action, or action of brute force, physical or psychical, either takes place between two subjects [whether they react equally upon each other, or one is agent and the other patient, entirely or partially] or at any rate is a resultant of such actions between pairs. But by "semiosis" I mean, on the contrary, an action, or influence, which is, or involves, a coöperation of *three* subjects, such as a sign, its object, and its interpretant, this tri-relative influence not being in any way resolvable into actions between pairs. . . .)[8]

Peirce's "tri-relative" notion of semiosis places him close to Frege, to Carnap, and to Ogden and Richards and far from Saussure and his followers. We can display their terminologies in the following way, placing the comparable (but by no means identical) terms of each formulation in the same column:

Frege	Expression (*Ausdruck*)	Sense (*Sinn*)	Reference (*Bedeutung*)
Carnap	Expression	Intension	Extension
Ogden/Richards	Symbol	Thought	Referent
Peirce	Sign	Interpretant	Object
Saussure	Signifier	Signified	———

The Saussurean formulation, like many "linguistic" views of language, eliminates the third term and with this gesture erases the world. For Saussure this was perhaps mainly a methodological convenience, a way of concentrating on the aspects of language that interested him. For deconstruction, however, this erasure of the world is crucial. The deconstructive critics argue that reference is a mirage of language, that there is no simple reference or unmediated perception, that the world is always already textualized by an archewriting or system of differentiation that effectively brackets or sets aside questions of reference, eliminating the terms in the third column not by choice but by necessity. It is this view that leads Derrida to say, "I don't know what perception is and I don't believe that anything like perception exists" (*The Structuralist Controversy*, ed. Macksey and Donato, p. 272).[9]

Derrida's statement, resplendent with Gallic hyperbole as it is, is simply a version of the more measured presentation of this view in *Speech and Phenomena*.[10] This is, in fact, the major position articulated in that critique of Husserl, and the foundation of all Derrida's later thought—and hence of the whole deconstructive enterprise:

> In affirming that *perception does not exist* or that what is called perception is not primordial, that somehow [*d'une certaine manière*] everything "begins" by "re-presentation" . . . and by reintroducing the difference involved in "signs" at the core of what is "primordial" . . . we are here indicating the prime

intention—and the ultimate scope—of the present essay. [SP, p. 45, n. 4, italics in original; gloss of "somehow" from *La voix et le phénomene*, p. 50]

At this stage of Derrida's thought he is content to call "signs" what he will elsewhere appropriate as "writing," but the point is unmistakable. There is no direct perception because what we perceive is always a sign of the thing rather than the thing itself.

This crucial point is based upon a theory of time. By denying that there is such a thing as "present time," Derrida can logically implicate the denial of presence itself. If we are never in the present, nothing can ever be present to us. Therefore, we never perceive anything. Culler explains it this way:

> Consider, for example, the flight of an arrow. If reality is what is present at any given *instant*, the arrow produces a paradox. At any given *moment* it is in a particular spot; it is always in a particular spot and never in motion. We want to insist, quite justifiably, that the arrow *is* in motion at every *instant* from the beginning to the end of its flight, yet its motion is never present at any moment of presence. The presence of motion is conceivable, it turns out, only insofar as every *instant* is already marked with traces of the past and the future. [*OD*, p. 94, italics of temporal terms added]

This is Zeno's paradox, adapted by Culler to illustrate Derrida's attack on presence. As you can see, it depends entirely upon the undefined concept of "instant" or "moment." How long is an instant? Even more important, who determines how long it is? Clearly, the notion is *not* grounded in human experience. It is a notion of time like the notion of a point in geometry: an ideal concept, not a real one. This is, in fact, the moment at which idealism enters the deconstructive system. From this point on, it is pervasive.

The point is worth dwelling upon. If the experience of the arrow were conceived in terms of the duration of its flight, one would have to admit that motion was perceivable. Even a camera, depending upon its exposure time, might record a blur of motion that had taken place during the "instant" in which its shutter was open. It is only by arbitrarily deciding that an instant is brief enough to miss the flight of the arrow that one can maintain that the arrow does not move during that instant. Even objects that move so fast they are beneath the threshold of human perception might appear motionless if captured in a brief enough unit of time. But to whom would they appear? All talk about human perception has got to reckon with the actual mechanisms of that perception or it is metaphysical in the worst sense of that word. But the Derridean instant, as presented by Culler, has nothing to do with human time and therefore nothing to do with human perception. It is a philosopher's paradox, pure and simple.

Upon this paradox, however, rests the entire theory of deconstruction, which asserts that we never experience anything because we encounter only deferred traces of things—or, more precisely, traces of traces: "The arbitrary nature of the sign and the system with no positive terms," says Culler, "give us the paradoxical notion of an 'instituted trace,' a structure of infinite referral in which there are only traces—traces prior to any entity of which they might be the trace" (OD, p. 99). Derrida himself has been explicit in linking his theory of traces to a theory of language:

> Whether in written or in spoken discourse, no element can function as a sign without relating to another element which is itself not simply present. This linkage means that each "element"—phoneme or grapheme—is constituted with reference to the trace in it of other elements of the sequence or system. [*Positions*, p. 26, quoted in OD, p. 99]

We should note a number of problems in this formulation: first, the deft substitution of talk about the signifier for talk about the whole sign; second the curious notion that every trace has "in it" traces of other elements. Does a trace have an inside? Derrida is forced to this curious usage because he is trying to avoid introducing the human mind as the instrument which relates one trace to another. To avoid the mind he has to speak of one trace as *present* inside another, and a very metaphysical presence it is. The final problem introduced in this brief discussion of the trace lies in the terms "sequence or system" in the last sentence. Nowhere in deconstructive discourse does any apologist for this position explain how sequence or system can be introduced into an aggregation of pure differences. When Saussure or Culler begin to talk specifically about language they always and inevitably introduce notions of similarity or hierarchy into the discussion. The deconstructionists tell us that every trace refers to every other trace and to nothing else, producing "a structure of infinite referral in which there are only traces" (*OD*, p. 99). If this were true, (a) it would not be a "structure," and (b) we would never know which trace we were encountering, since they would all be alike. If we cannot perceive things, we cannot perceive phonemes or graphemes, either, since they are things, too.

In discussing Saussure as Derrida's predecessor, Culler must finally admit that Saussure's treatment of language diverges significantly from Derrida's. He does this by accusing Saussure of logocentrism, which, of course, Derrida has transcended:

> The concept of the sign is so involved with the basic concepts of logocentrism that it would be difficult for Saussure to shift it even if he wished to. Though much of his analysis does work to that end, he explicitly affirms a logocentric conception of the sign and thus inscribes his analysis within logocentrism. [*OD*, p. 99]

The implications of inscribing one's analysis within logocentrism obviously include the possibility of inscribing oneself somewhere else, but it is not easy to say where this is. There is something wrong, Culler tells us, with the "concept of the sign itself," because it subordinates the signifier to "the concept or meaning that it communicates" (*OD*, p. 99). Culler presents Saussure as struggling with a tangle of concepts ("The *concept* of the sign is so involved with the basic *concepts* of logocentrism") almost too heavy to shift. But Saussure was not simply struggling with concepts. He was trying to describe the way languages work in reality. Deconstruction, of course, denies the premises of linguistic science and all the other sciences. All attempts to get at realities, whether physical or social, are inscribed within logocentrism. The denial of all possibility of perception involves the further denial of all evidence based upon observation or measurement. There is no appeal open from thought to experience, because there is no experience.

Saussure, however, thought he was a scientist. My quarrel with him is precisely the opposite of Culler's. I find that his definition of the sign as a sound-image and a concept is inadequate to describe those elements in language that depend upon the relationship between concepts and objects or referents. His definition of the sign is deficient not because it gives the concept too much weight but because it ignores the referent entirely. Reference, as even W. V. O. Quine is happy to admit, is inscrutable. We can never know what another person is referring to, even if he points to an object as he speaks, because we can never know exactly what part or aspect of the object is being designated. But we cannot ignore reference and make any progress in learning a language. In fact, we make the same sort of distinctions among the objects of language as we do among the sounds or written words, settling for roughly the same referent, roughly the same concept, and roughly the same phoneme or grapheme. The linguist who gets too "cagey," as Quine puts it, will never be able to describe a language; "A cagey linguist is a caged linguist" (*Ontological Relativity*, p. 3).[11]

Returning to Saussure's example of *boeuf* and *Ochs*, it should be obvious that the very same animal (imagine it on the left bank of the Rhine, near Strasbourg) might be called both names by someone who points to it while teaching another person one of the two languages in question. In such a case, the identical object, indicated by the identical gesture, would be our measure of the near identity of the signifieds. Derrida would say that this is not so, that no act of perception is taking place. Quine would say that perception is taking place, all right, but that one can never be sure that any two people are perceiving exactly the same parts or aspects of the object before them, which makes the notion of reference problematic or, as he puts it, "inscrutable." Reference involves an interaction between perception and a "coordinate system" or, as we say, and Quine says, a "frame of reference" (*OR*, p. 48). Language, culture, our social frame of reference—all these exert a tremendous pressure on the selectivity of perception. But things are *there*, soliciting our attention. Living objects—animals that we herd or catch, see, smell, touch, hear, notice in motion, even eat—solicit our attention in a peculiar and extraordinarily insistent way, because we are animals, too. Language exists *in order* for us to talk about such things, among others. In every language there are words for certain things not because language has "chosen" arbitrarily to create those words but because the things were sufficiently *there* to force language to accommodate them. To make this process as graphic as possible, I propose to consider two cases in which objects hitherto absent from the English language appeared and were perceived, establishing a referent/signified relationship before a signified/signifier relationship in English could be generated. What we find in these cases, as in many other cases of nominalization in all languages, is that the signifiers may be arbitrary but the signifieds are motivated by reference, which flows not only from the word to the thing but from the thing to the word.

It is not easy to find the exact points at which nontechnical words have entered the English language. The moment always seems to elude us. But there is one beautiful specimen of this, from which we can learn a good deal. I refer to the word *kangaroo*. We know with great and unusual precision when this word entered the language, but we have no idea where the signifier itself came from. The referents, however, were hopping around Captain James Cook when he landed at Botany Bay, Australia, in 1770. There they were, plainly perceptible, and totally devoid of English signifiers. A strict deconstructionist, of course, would have to deny that they were perceptible at all. Since this is precisely the kind of example we never get in deconstructive discourse, it will be instructive to speculate upon how such an event would be considered by a deconstructor. Before being named would the kangaroos have been invisible? How would this "non-perception" (the term is Derrida's) of them have occurred? Specifically, to what extent would it be proper to say that the explorers were encountering traces *of* kangaroos as opposed to traces of non-kangaroos or traces of other traces. The question may sound silly, but its implications are serious. I would want to describe this process in terms of a sensory sign, a sign motivated by the stimulation of human visual and mental processes (among others)—by, for instance, the transmission of light rays from a present kangaroo to the eyes of the explorers. The strict deconstructionist would have to deny this all along the line. No presence, therefore no transmission of light rays, and therefore no set of visual images in the mind of the observer. The signs or traces that later came to be connected with the English signifier "kangaroo" could not be iconic, could not be images *of* kangaroos. This is why deconstruction always ignores the existence of iconic signs. But let us return to the verbal signifier.

Legend has it that a member of Cook's party asked a native of the newly discovered continent (a whopping new signified in itself) what these things were called, and the native replied with a set of sounds that the English perceived as "kangaroo," taking that to be the name of the beast, though it actually meant "Damned if I know," or signifieds to that effect. Legend, as usual, is impossible to substantiate. Later investigators have failed to find any language in which something that sounds like "kangaroo" means either the proper animal or "I don't know." But signifier and signified have lived happily together in the English language ever after.

Throughout the centuries of its history the English language never chose to exercise its arbitrary right to generate the linguistic sign "kangaroo" until a certain day in 1770 when the concept hopped into an English mind demanding a name. The whole episode is unpleasantly similar to the account of the naming of animals in the Book of Genesis, for which I apologize, and strikingly different from the process of arbitrary signification attributed to Saussure. I take it that, logically speaking, one case like this is enough to show that the "Saussurean" account is imperfect, but the ramifications of the issue are far too important to allow the whole case to rest upon this single instance. Part of what is at stake will become visible if I ask a question about kangaroos. Were there any kangaroos before 1770? That is, were they *there* whether the English language recognized them or not? If you think the answer is obvious, think again. Personally, I believe they were there. I believe that the world is full of things that, as Charles Peirce said, are the way they are "regardless of what you or I may think about it." The apologists for deconstruction do not believe this, for their mode of thought is thoroughly imbued with idealism. Consider, for example, these words of Barbara Johnson, in the excellent introduction to her quite extraordinary translation of Derrida's *La dissemination*:

> Copernicus can be said to have written a critique of the Ptolemaic conception of the universe. But the idea that the earth goes around the sun is not an *improvement* of the idea that the sun goes around the earth. It is a shift in perspective that literally makes the ground move. [*Dissemination*, p. xx][12]

From the perspective of deconstruction, there is nothing upon which we can ground an argument for evolutionary biology as opposed to fundamentalist creationism, since both are discourses, with their blindness and their insights, and neither one can be said to be more or less accurate than the other, there being no pathway open from the text to the world. The issue of whether or not signifieds are purely arbitrary or partly grounded upon phenomena is an issue of great consequence.

The kangaroo example is too simple to stand on its own. It needs, at the very least, a tale to prop it up. Let us consider a comparable situation with a different result. Here is a passage from Aphra Behn's novella of 1688, *Oroonoko*:

> At other times he would go a Fishing; and discoursing on that Diversion, he found we had in that Country a very strange Fish, call'd a *Numb-Eel*, (an *Eel* of which I have eaten) that while it is alive, it has a Quality so cold, that those who are angling tho' with a Line of ever so great a Length, with a Rod at the End of it, it shall in the same Minute the Bait is touched by this *Eel*, seize him or her that holds the Rod with a Numbness, that shall deprive 'em of Sense for a While.[13]

This bizarre fictional event is set in Surinam, in the West Indies, a place in which Aphra Behn lived for some years before becoming what Lionel Stevenson called "the first professional authoress." The episode of the Numb-Eel has been dismissed by a recent critic as simply "another wonder" in a novel "steeped in an insecurity resulting from bad faith, criminality, lying, and fabrication."[14] It is judgments of this severity, perhaps, that drive people to deconstruction, but there is no doubt that Mrs. Behn is writing fiction. Still, that Eel bothers me.

In the episode of the Eel, Caesar (the slave-name of Oroonoko, the royal slave) goes fishing, is numbed, falls into the river, supported by his rod, with an Eel still caught on his hook. When some Indians in a boat try to help him, "a Numbness" seizes them, until they push the rod away from Caesar with their paddle, lifting it and the Eel into their boat with this paddle, and then rescue Caesar easily with their hands. It is a "wonder" of sorts, but I sense behind it a reality trying to enter the English consciousness through a language ill-prepared to receive it. More than half a century before Ben Franklin flew his kite, when the word "electricity" was used only by a few savants like Sir Thomas Browne to signify something like the phenomena we know as magnetic attraction and static electricity, a young Englishwoman in South America encountered signs of what we now call electric eels. Perhaps she did eat one. That the "wonder" she has given us bears so many indices of the phenomenon of electricity as we now know it, from current flow broken by a wooden paddle to the numbing effect of electric shock—an experience no natural philosopher in Europe had yet encountered—and all this connected to a sort of eel in precisely the part of the world where these eels have continued to be found—makes this wonder even more wonderful: a strange new signified, swimming into the mind of woman, seeking a signifier that can't quite come into being. Unlike the word "kangaroo," "Numb-Eel" never found its place in the English language, and "electric eel" had to wait for a more developed concept of electricity before it could take shape as a signifier for this strange fish.

What this example demonstrates, I believe, is that in the naming function of language (the only one we are really discussing here) there is pressure and resistance on both sides of the signified. Experience, whether or not it is mediated by an arche-writing, presents to our languaging faculty more finished possibilities than Saussure admits to his system. In his chapter on linguistic value, which is one of the most valuable in the *Course*, Saussure argues that,

> Psychologically our thought—apart from its expression in words—is only a shapeless and indistinct mass. Philosophers and linguists have always agreed in recognizing that without the help of signs we would be unable to make a clear-cut, consistent distinction between two ideas. Without language, thought is a vague, uncharted nebula. There are no pre-existing ideas, and nothing is distinct before the appearance of language. [*CGL*, pp. 111–12]

This is the heart of Saussure's doctrine. It argues powerfully for the dependence of thought upon language, but there is a flaw of enormous consequence in the argument as it is presented here. The flaw is in the shift from "signs" to "language" between the second and the third sentences. The phrase "without the help of *signs*" in one sentence is repeated as "without *language*" in the next. The problem has two dimensions, which we can formulate as two questions: (1) Are all signs linguistic signs? (2) Are linguistic signs purely linguistic—that is, are verbal meanings sustained entirely by relations among words or are relations with nonverbal entities also involved? Saussure, Derrida, and their followers like to go as far as possible in the direction of answering both of those questions affirmatively. One stratagem is to close down the opening to the nonverbal allowed by Saussure when he defined semiology as including the study of "natural signs." Derrida does this by supplanting semiology with grammatology, essentially reducing all sign processes to "writing." Saussure himself does it by insisting that "signs that are wholly arbitrary realize better than the others the ideal of the semiological process" (*CGL*, p. 68). And Culler does it in a very revealing way:

> Various typologies of signs have been proposed, but three fundamental classes of signs seem to stand out as requiring different approaches: the icon, the index, and the sign proper (sometimes misleadingly called "symbol"). . . .
> What are the implications of this three-way division for semiology? The main consequence is to make the sign proper the central object of semiology and to make the study of other signs a specialized and secondary activity. [*FS*, p. 104]

In this passage Culler not only suppresses the name of Charles Peirce, whose work is the source of these "fundamental classes" of signs; he also appropriates the name of "sign" for one of the three classes. The "sign proper" is the sign based on an arbitrary system of pure differences: the proper sign is the pure sign, the verbal sign, the word. But this relegation of impure or motivated signs to a "specialized and secondary activity" can purify semiotics only by crippling it. Eliminating maps, diagrams, painting, sculpture, film, ideogram, hieroglyph, and all other motivated ways of signifying from the domain of semiology can hardly strengthen the field. All it can accomplish is to maintain the artificial purity of the purely differential sign, a purity that is not even found in the verbal realm of dictionaries, where iconic signs are often used to explain verbal ones. Nor does such purity obtain in our mental lexicons, where visual, kinetic, and tactile signifieds are regularly linked to verbal signifiers. Think of "triangle," "spiral," and "toothache," for instance. Or "kangaroo." Language is neither proper nor pure.

Saussure presents a number of elegant and persuasive examples of the way that "within the same language, all words used to express related ideas limit each other reciprocally" (*CGL*, p. 116). What he does not explain is how "related" ideas are, in fact, related. And this is the problem upon which his theory—and all others that accept it uncritically—have foundered. Saussure's term for this relationship is usually "association"—another term that connects him to John Locke. This term has been suppressed by his structuralist and post-structuralist apologists. Even the compilers of the index to both the French and American editions of the *Course* have ignored the fact that Chapter V of Part II is entitled "Syntagmatic and Associative Relations" ("Rapports Syntagmatiques et Rapports Associatifs").

The term "paradigmatic," which is usually substituted for Saussure's "associative," is simply another way of glossing over a problem instead of glossing it. "A particular word," Saussure tells us, "is like the center of a constellation; it is the point of convergence of an indefinite number of co-ordinated terms" (*CGL*, p. 126). The question is, how are these terms "coordinated"? Saussure is quite clear on the matter at this point in his text, though it conflicts with what he seems to be saying at other points. Here, he tells us that words "that have something in common are associated in the memory." Such "associations may spring from the analogy of the concepts signified . . . or, again, simply from the similarity of the sound images" (*CGL*, pp. 125–26). Once again, we must ask about the basis for any "analogy among the concepts." What is the mechanism which allows "memory" to link "analogous" concepts despite the "arbitrary" differences in their respective sound-images, and despite the supposed fact that language is a "system of pure differences." David Hume could help us here: "To me there appear to be only three principles of connexion among ideas, namely, *Resemblance, Contiguity* in time or place, and *Cause* or *Effect*."[15] If Hume is right, the major figures of rhetoric are grounded upon these "principles of connexion," which are universal and therefore innate features of human mental processes. Hume may well be wrong, but at least he gives us a way of beginning to consider how signifieds are organized in paradigmatic relations.

Saussure is always dependent upon such connections, even when he pretends he is not. Some of his most celebrated examples of difference are convincing only because he has assumed an encompassing association, as in his discussion of French *mouton* as opposed to English sheep *and* mutton. A Frenchman can either raise or eat *mouton*, but an Englishman must raise sheep and eat mutton. Thus the English term *sheep* has a different "value" than the French term *mouton*, because it has the second term, *mutton*, "beside it." How does the term *mutton* get "beside" the term *sheep*, anyway? What connects them? What connects the term *wool* to the term sheep? Why is *mutton* closer to *sheep* than *beef* would be? Saussure tries to sustain a distinction between the "signification" of a word and its "value," claiming that French *mouton* and English *sheep* have the same signification but different values, but this distinction proves impossible to explain, let alone sustain.

The insistence on the arbitrariness of the sign, in the hands of Saussure's followers, has come to mean the total independence of verbal signs from nonverbal signs and, of course, from any state of affairs that is not determined by the purely differential system that language is supposed to be. To some extent—even to a great extent—this has been a useful corrective to naive empiricisms of all sorts. Language is *not* transparent upon reality. Agreed. Perception is not unmediated, either. Agreed. But one cannot say even these things without claiming knowledge. Some time ago Bertrand Russell alerted us to "the position of language in the world of fact. Language consists of sensible phenomena just as much as eating or walking, and if we can know nothing about facts we cannot know what other people say or even what we are saying ourselves" (*My Philosophical Development*, p. 110). Personally, I would insist that language consists of insensible structures that are inferred from the sensible phenomena of writing and speech, but I accept the main point. Texts are just as much a part of the world as kangaroos or atomic submarines. If we are totally cut off from things, language must be one of the things from which we are cut off. If, on the other hand, we can think about texts with any degree of effectiveness, we can think about other things effectively, too.

I am trying to undo, or at least cast doubt upon, the fundamental structuralist and post-structuralist view of language as a system of pure differences. Despite their numerous assertions that language is indeed purely differential, in their actual illustrations of pure difference at work Saussure and his followers regularly reveal that language is always already contaminated by human perception and reference. Jonathan Culler, for instance, offers us an elegant demonstration of the ways in which the English and French languages have terms for flowing bodies of water (river, stream, *rivière, fleuve*) that make different conceptual distinctions: a river is larger than a stream; a *fleuve* may or may not be larger than a *rivière*, but it flows into the sea and a *rivière* does not. Culler uses this illustration to demonstrate that, "Not only can a language arbitrarily choose its signifiers; it can divide up a spectrum of conceptual possibilities in any way it likes" (*FS*, p. 16). Once again, language is personified and allowed to have a free choice in selecting signifiers. But the selection is from a "spectrum of conceptual possibilities," that is to say, a set of possibilities already *selected out* of the immense total of conceptual possibilities, selected out by an iconic similitude that ultimately depends upon nonlinguistic states of affairs. "Obviously it is important that a language have ways of talking about flowing bodies of water," says Culler, "but it can make its conceptual distinctions in this area in a wide variety of ways" (*FS*, p. 16). This freedom of language to "divide up a spectrum," as Culler puts it, is obviously dependent upon the prior recognition of the spectrum itself as an already organized set of conceptual possibilities. The "spectrum" is differentiated from the immense total of all conceptual possibilities by the similarity among the possibilities included in this particular spectrum. Wherever we look in language, we will find difference *and* similarity in mutual dependency, just as we will find conceptual material organized in ways that are partly random and partly determined by the interaction of human perceptual systems with the human environment. It is important to talk "about flowing bodies of water" because they are *there*. The Eskimos have more concepts for snow than the Bedouins not because their language has "chosen" to have them but because their experience has necessitated a more discriminated understanding of snow. Perhaps we can lay the myth of pure difference to rest if we consider the one dimension of language in which the notion of a "spectrum" of conceptual possibilities is not a metaphor.

"Color terms," says Culler, "are a particularly good example" of the way in which signs are defined by other members of the system to which they belong. He demonstrates this by supposing a situation in which one wishes to teach "a rather slow learner . . . from a non-European culture" about "colors in English." The wrong way to do this, Culler suggests, would be to start with one color, brown, show him a hundred brown things, and then expect him to identify all the brown objects in a room. He would fail this test, Culler assures us, because he will never understand what brown is "until he has grasped the relation between brown and other colors," because brown is "not an independent concept defined by some essential properties but one term in a system of color terms, defined by its relations with the other terms which delimit it" (*FS*, pp. 16–17). There is certainly some truth in this view, but the example of colors seems singularly ill chosen to illustrate the purity of linguistic differentiation. We have only to imagine another experiment in which we introduce our slow-learning non-European to all the "color terms" in the English language but with no visual representation of any color at all: no brown objects or samples of brown paint, etc. Our subject would have all the words. How do you think he would fare in picking out the brown objects? The point is a simple but important one. A visual image is a part of the meaning of every color term. Without such an image the signifiers lack the major component of their signifieds, which in fact depend upon reference. Wittgenstein can help us see what is at stake here:

> 13. Imagine a *tribe* of colour-blind people, and there could easily be one. They would not have the same colour concepts as we do. For even assuming they speak, e.g. English, and thus have all the English colour words, they would still use them differently than we do and would *learn* their use differently.
> Or if they have a foreign language, it would be difficult for us to translate their colour words into ours. [*Remarks on Colour*][16]

This language game points toward the difficulties in a purely verbal view of language. Culler is quite correct to argue that different languages may divide up the color spectrum differently, but it is the same spectrum that is being divided up: "same" in the sense that it is given by mechanisms of sense perception that show no significant difference across language barriers. The problem changes if we assume either a different world or a different mechanism of color perception. W. V. O. Quine has usefully considered the question of different mechanisms of color perception, pointing out that social pressures can induce a generalized norm for use of the word "red" even by a color-blind person, but insisting that even the color-blind will be relying upon sensory stimuli in using the word. We can usefully set Quine's formulation of the signifying process against Saussure's:

> The uniformity that unites us in communication and belief is a uniformity of resultant patterns overlying a chaotic subjective diversity of connections between words and experience. [*Word and Object*, p. 8][17]

Quine's emphasis on "experience" is what distinguishes his view from Saussure's. The verbal sign does indeed bring a social order out of a subjective chaos for both writers, but Saussure's chaos is a chaos of thought ("the floating realm of thought"); Quine's is a chaos of experience. Quine also points out that the experiential chaos is at its minimal extent with respect to color terms like "red," which he calls "a happy case where a nearly uniform stimulatory condition is shared by simultaneous observers" (*WO*, p. 7).

The question of how colors would appear in a different world altogether has been taken up by Wittgenstein:

> 42. We will, therefore, have to ask ourselves: What would it be like if people knew colours which our people with normal vision do not know? In general this question will not admit of an unambiguous answer. For it is by no means clear that we must say of this sort of abnormal people that they know other *colours*. There is, after all, no commonly accepted criterion for what is a colour, unless it is one of our colours.
>
> And yet we could imagine circumstances under which we would say, "These people see other colours in addition to ours." [*Remarks on Colour*]

As it happens, in 1920 a writer of fiction imagined a world in which a normal Englishman encounters other colors and attempts to describe them in English. The result is a language game as instructive as Wittgenstein's:

> It was an entirely new color—not a shade or combination, but a new primary color, as vivid as blue, red or yellow, but quite different. When he inquired, she told him that it was known as "ulfire." Presently he met with a second new color. This she designated "jale." The sense impressions caused in Maskull by these two additional primary colors can only be vaguely hinted at by analogy. Just as blue is delicate and mysterious, yellow clear and unsubtle, and red sanguine and passionate, so he felt ulfire to be wild and painful, and jale dreamlike, feverish, and voluptuous.[18]

"Jale" and "ulfire" have been introduced into English, here, and one could even put them grammatically into other sentences, but, as Wittgenstein might ask, could they be considered color terms in the same sense as red, yellow, and blue? Could we use them in the same way as the other color terms, with the same amount of consistency, the same potential for nuance? If they were to become part of the English language—as they have not in the more than sixty years since they first were used—how would they fare, without the support of the visual interpretants that determine the meanings of the color terms we normally use?

The lessons we learn from considering the necessary visual aspects of color terms must be extended to everything in language that is partly determined by sensory data. Perception is impure, and certainly contaminated by language. But language is impure, too, and certain aspects of linguistic meaning are heavily dependent upon nonlinguistic forms of information. Umberto Eco has put it this way:

> The compositional analysis of a verbal term should not consider as its interpretants only linguistic terms. Among the interpretants of the word "red" are also images of red objects or a red cue as the specific space within the graduated continuum of the chromatic spectrum. Among the interpretants of the word "dog" are all the images of dogs displayed by encyclopedias, zoological treatises, and all the comic strips in which that word has been associated to these images and vice versa. . . . No semantic analysis can be complete without analyzing verbal expressions by means of visual, objectal, and behavioral interpretants, and vice versa. [*The Role of the Reader*, pp. 196–97]

Eco's formulation, which I entirely endorse, can be set against the deconstructive view we have been examining. The major difference is that in Eco's semiotic view, the verbal and nonverbal worlds are held to be interdependent. In deconstructive discourse, on the contrary, great pains are taken to insist that there be no trafficking between words and pictures, even, let alone words and things. Only "arbitrary" or linguistic signs are "signs proper." In short, much of the deconstructive enterprise rests upon a major act of appropriation, the exclusion of what Eco calls the "visual, the objectal, and the behavioral" from the domain of "signs proper," which is restricted to the grapho-centric world of the written word, purified by the expulsion of all nonverbal features.

The deconstructive position supports the hermetic view of textuality, and the hermetic view of textuality inhibits any attempt to criticize either a text or the world. For these reasons I think we must reject those elements of deconstruction that support the hermetic theory of texts. In doing so, however, we should take care to salvage those other features of deconstruction that can in fact enhance secular criticism, enabling feminists and other socially committed writers to obtain textual power over their worlds. In the next chapter we shall consider two ways in which this has been done.

7

THE LEFT HAND OF DIFFERENCE

> . . . the most profound region of pheno-
> menological reflection, where darkness
> risks being no longer the provision of
> appearing or the field which offers itself
> to phenomenal light, but the forever noc-
> turnal source of the light itself.
>
> Jacques Derrida,
> *Introduction to Husserl's "Origin
> of Geometry"*

> In the tale, in the telling, we are all one
> blood. Take the tale in your teeth, then,
> and bite till the blood runs . . . and we
> will all come to the end together, and
> even to the beginning: living, as we do,
> in the middle.
>
> Ursula K. LeGuin,
> "It Was a Dark and Stormy Night"

The strict deconstructionist case, as I argued in the previous chapter, is far from perfect, yet a lot of interesting critical work has been done in the name of deconstruction, especially by Derrida himself. What I have objected to in deconstruction is the attempt to deny absolutely both perception and reference on the grounds of their imperfection. Throughout this book I am struggling to maintain some middle ground between the absolute denial of reference and perception, on the one hand, and the absolute refusal to understand perception and reference as problematic, on the other. The position I take all along, sometimes arguing one side of the case, sometimes the other, is that we neither capture nor create the world with our texts, but interact with it. Human language intervenes in a world that has already intervened in language. We divide the world into classes of things: trees, bushes, shrubs, flowers, weeds, and vegetables, for instance, which need not be divided up in just that way. But neither we as individuals, nor our cultural group, nor yet language itself can accomplish this division freely and arbitrarily. The world resists language as the grain of a tree resists the saw, and saws take the form they do partly because wood is what it is. We sense the presence of things through this resistance. But, as with the saw, language differentiates by an act of violence. This view, common to both structuralists and deconstructionists, seems to me very persuasive. I, too, believe that violence and alienation are aspects of the price we pay for the textual power of language. Human beings become human through the acquisition of language, and this acquisition alienates humans from all those things that language names. The name is a substitute for the thing; it displaces the thing in the very act of naming it, so that language finally stands even between one human being and another. Much of our poetry has been written to undo this condition, to remove the veil of language that covers everything with a false familiarity, to (in the words of the Russian formalist Viktor Shklovsky) "make the stone stoney," or, failing this, to at least make language itself visible: to make the word wordy.

Starting from this position we can examine all our uses of language from a new point of view, not to see what they reveal but to consider what they conceal, and to ask the question, "What violence is being done here?" The most basic and most violent acts of differentiation are those that divide a field into two opposed units. This sort of "binary opposition," as the structuralists call it, is fundamental to the phonemic structure of speech and is deeply embedded in all Western thought, whether logical or mythical. How many times a day and in how many situations do we find ourselves thinking in terms of good and bad, insiders and outsiders, us and them? And how much do we conceal, even from ourselves—especially from ourselves—when we use those categories in our habitual way?

One of our most important binary oppositions, of course, is the opposition between male and female, which seems to so embody the principle of differentiation that it moved an irrepressible Frenchman to cry aloud, "Vive la différence!" More recently, Jacques Derrida has been moved to offer us a variant on that word: "différance," spelled -*ance* but, in accordance with the rules of French pronunciation, spoken in exactly the same way as its predecessor. Derrida has made this move for several reasons. By changing the spelling and the meaning without changing the pronunciation, he has sought to emphasize the importance of writing in relation to speech, and to question or problematize the notion of difference itself. This new notion of *differance* is what the philosophers call a "term of art" (which I will here treat in a somewhat artless and superficial way). One of its principal functions is to remind us of that basic act of differentiation by which language offers us control of things at the price of distancing us from them. And one of its most powerful implications is that this initial difference operates to make every verbal formula incomplete, requiring a perpetual supplementary activity, a de-constructing of language by means of more language.

How language can deconstruct language has thus become an acute problem for both theory and practice. Derrida himself has tried various means, using words under erasure, as he says, crossing them out but leaving them in place; he has encouraged all sorts of playfulness; he and his followers have privileged the fragment as a literary form, have set up systems of multiple textuality, with different texts competing on the same page, and have approved all sorts of disruptive efforts in an attempt to dislodge traditional literary and linguistic practice. Above all, the deconstructive critics have sought to mount critiques of those binary oppositions used to organize fields or systems of value in traditional kinds of writing. These critiques take the form of bringing the oppositions to light, showing how power and privilege are often surreptitiously mapped onto apparently neutral

oppositions, and finally dismantling or deconstructing oppositions by showing how each term shares certain attributes with its
opposite, or presenting cases that the opposition cannot assimi-
late. A basic cultural binary opposition that has frequently received deconstructive attention but proved singularly intractable
is the difference between male and female.

The distinction between male and female is especially important because it seems to be one of those instances where
language merely names a difference that is already *there* in
nature, written into terrestrial genetic coding as it is into the
Book of Genesis. But nature is itself a culturally determined
category, held in place by culture in the binary opposition:
nature/culture. We do not consider everything that is produced by nature natural. If the genetic codes produce a creature of anomalous or conflated sexuality we will say that nature
has made a mistake and send her back to the old drawing
board. The categories of language are absolute in their rage for
differentiation.

Nowhere is language more absolute than in its treatment of
sexuality. In English we distinguish only three categories in our
third person singular personal pronouns: males, females, and
things either sexless or indeterminate. We may refer to a dog as
"it," but if we know the sex, we say "he" or "she." Even an
altered tomcat will often get a courtesy "he." We can refer to a
baby as "it" without great distress, but we cannot so refer to a
full-grown human being. We *must* say "he" or "she" unless we
mean to be extremely insulting, and we had better get the he and
she of it right unless we want to be terribly embarrassed. In
short, the categorical opposition male/female is built into our
language, and therefore into our thought, at the very deepest
level, the level of pronominal reference.

The linguistic categories male and female are not only more
absolute than any natural differences and more pervasive, they
are also loaded with cultural baggage, much of which is highly
invidious. From the Pythagoreans to the Renaissance—a matter
of two millennia—much of Western thought was influenced by a

list of oppositions made popular by Aristotle. The list, as Ian MacLean has reproduced it in *The Renaissance Notion of Woman*[1], presents two columns of opposites, with the left-hand column clearly the favored or privileged set:

male	female
limit	unlimited
odd	even
one	plurality
right	left
square	oblong
at rest	moving
straight	curved
light	darkness
good	evil

Many things can be said about this fascinating cultural paradigm. Most obviously, we can note that the left-hand column begins with male and ends with good; the right-hand column begins with female and ends with evil. We can note that Verdi's wicked count in *Rigoletto*, who sings that woman is changeable or moveable *(mobile)*, is simply uniting two terms from the right-hand column of this paradigm. We could find many other cases of literary texts that are rooted in this rich matrix of patriarchal pride and prejudice. For our purposes, however, the important combination of terms from the right-hand column is "left" and "darkness." That a book which explores and questions traditional thinking about masculinity and femininity should be called *The Left Hand of Darkness*[2] is clearly significant, and one thing that it signifies is a deliberate effort to mount a critique of a paradigmatic system of binary oppositions.

I do not wish to suggest that Ursula K. LeGuin is a Derridean or a programmatic deconstructivist writer; only to observe that she is working in the same space, for many of the same ends, and having a good deal of success, for reasons that I think I can explain. One of the great difficulties in mounting a critique of values that seem to be embedded both in language and in human flesh is getting outside of language and outside of the world we think we know. One route outside is by way of a special technical language or a repertory of disruptive devices. The other way is by imagining another world. We might call the first Derrida's Way and the second LeGuin's Way. There are those who think both things can and should be done at the same time—and perhaps this is so. But they can hardly be done at the same time if one wishes to reach a wide audience. LeGuin's Way involves working in a popular genre, accepting many of the norms of that genre and of the English language, and there is a price to pay for that kind of compromise. But there is a price for refusing to compromise, too.

In *The Left Hand of Darkness* LeGuin is working at the end of the genre of science fiction that is closest to the utopian didactic form of fiction established in England by Thomas More. She has accepted the constraints of her popular genre—to tell a rousing story based on a condition contrary to the arrangements of our world but compatible with what we believe about our world's possible transformations. Her contrary condition is a simple but powerful one. She proposes to us a world populated by human beings who are like us in every respect save one: they are all hermaphrodites, all androgynes. This is the situation on "Winter" or "Gethen," the alternate world presented to us in *The Left Hand of Darkness*. But to understand more fully her accomplishment and its implications we must back up a bit and consider how this project was undertaken.

In 1969 a story by LeGuin appeared in *Orbit 5*, under the title "Winter's King." It was about highly sophisticated mind control through drugs and hypnosis, used as a political weapon on a planet undergoing an ice age—a planet known as "Winter" to those from gentler worlds. This planet was to become the location of *The Left Hand of Darkness*, but, as LeGuin has observed, when she wrote the story she "did not know that the inhabitants of the planet were androgynes" (*The Wind's Twelve Quarters*, p. 93).[3] This knowledge came later, as she began work on the novel. She speaks of its as "knowledge," using the novelist's privilege of referring to inventions as discoveries, in the manner of Balzac, but perhaps she is simply speaking a truth. We forget, sometimes, that when we attribute total freedom of choice to an artist we are constructing a fiction of freedom, projecting our own needs and desires upon a figure who is far less free than we may assume.

For our purposes, however, the important point is that androgyny became a central element in the world of the novel. There are several such elements that became the matrices out of which the whole fictional world is constructed: the coldness of the climate, the political division of this world into two states—one feudal, one totalitarian—and the element of androgyny. There is also a story to be told, a story of human relationship and of adventure. I propose to ignore all these matters except one—androgyny—and to consider the others only as they relate to that one.

The established norms of the genre—a condition contrary to present fact but in harmony with present scientific theory—can be seen operating throughout LeGuin's novel. Androgyny is the major condition contrary to the facts of our lives, though the occasional hermaphrodites born into the human species are a kind of justification for extending this possibility to a whole race of human beings. In the novel it is suggested that this race did not occur naturally but was in fact the result of a deliberate genetic experiment. Other details are added in the text to bring this contrary condition further and further within the realm of scientific belief. The sexual cycle of these beings is not continuous, as in humans, but periodic, as in animals. The menstrual cycle of human females is in fact the model for the erotic cycle of all Gethenians. Every month they come into a brief period, like estrus in earthly mammals, in which they are sexually active. In the novel, the full explanation of all this comes in the form of a scientific report by an investigator from another world—a "normal" human being. Let me quote from this report:

The sexual cycle averages 26 to 28 days (they tend to speak of it as 26 days, approximating it to the lunar cycle). For 21 or 22

days the individual is *somer*, sexually inactive, latent. On about
the 18th day hormonal changes are initiated by the pituitary
control and on the 22nd or 23rd day the individual enters
kemmer, estrus. In this first phase of kemmer (Karh. *secher*) he
remains completely androgynous. Gender, and potency, are
not attained in isolation. A Gethenian in first-phase kemmer, if
kept alone or with others not in kemmer, remains incapable of
coitus. Yet the sexual impulse is tremendously strong in this
phase, controlling the entire personality, subjecting all other
drives to its imperative. When the individual first finds a partner in kemmer, hormonal secretion is further stimulated (most
importantly by touch—secretion? scent?) until in one partner
either a male or female hormonal dominance is established.
The genitals engorge or shrink accordingly, foreplay intensi-
fies, and the partner, triggered by the change, takes on the
other sexual role (?without exception? If there are exceptions,
resulting in kemmer-partners of the same sex, they are so
rare as to be ignored). This second phase of kemmer (Karh.
thorharmen), the mutual process of establishing sexuality and
potency, apparently occurs within a time-span of two to twenty
hours. If one of the partners is already in full kemmer, the phase
for the new partner is liable to be quite short; if the two are
entering kemmer together, it is likely to take longer. Normal
individuals have no predisposition to either sexual role in
kemmer; they do not know whether they will be the male or the
female, and have no choice in the matter. [*LHD*, pp. 65–66]

Presenting the information in the form of a scientific report
accomplishes a number of things. It justifies a whole chapter
of exposition, of course, getting the information to the reader
in the most compact way possible. It also brings this fantastic—
or potentially fantastic—element in the book firmly under the
rubric of science. This is the familiar discourse of science,
with questions, reservations, and a rather severe, technical
vocabulary.

So far, everything that we have considered has been in the
service of the generic constraints: a condition contrary to fact
made conformable to theory. But there is something else that

justifies science fiction as a genre, which many of the best works in that genre have achieved. The anomalous condition may throw a reflected light upon the very norms from which it departs. It enables us to *see* the system which it violates as we have never seen that system before. And in this case, the system that it lets us see is the system of sexual difference itself, and it lets us see this system in a way that no realistic work of fiction, however eloquent, could accomplish. It enables us to see the system of sexual difference *as* a system because it has offered us a *differance* from *difference*—a place to stand from which we can finally see the earth and perhaps even move it.

In that sober scientific report on the sexual behavior of the Gethenians, at a certain point the discussion shifts from biology to sociology. This happens as the scientist turns to the implications of this biology and in particular to the difficulty that "normal" human beings are going to have in comprehending this strange world. "Consider," she says:

> The fact that everyone between seventeen and thirty-five or so is liable to be (as Nim put it) "tied down to childbearing," implies that no one is quite so thoroughly "tied down" here as women, elsewhere, are likely to be—psychologically or physically. Burden and privilege are shared out pretty equally; everybody has the same risk to run or choice to make. Therefore nobody here is quite so free as a free male anywhere else. [p. 68]

And again, "Consider," she says: "A child has no psycho-sexual relationship to his mother and father. There is no myth of Oedipus on Winter" (p. 68). She adds:

> When you meet a Gethenian you cannot and must not do what a bisexual naturally does, which is to cast him in the role of Man or Woman, while adopting towards him a corresponding role dependent on your expectations of the patterned or possible interaction between persons of the same or the opposite sex. Our entire pattern of socio-sexual interaction is nonexistent here. They cannot play the game. They do not see one another

as men or women. This is almost impossible for our imagination to accept. What is the first question we ask about a newborn baby? [pp. 68–69]

This is science fiction with a strong element of the utopian didactic. It presents itself as a scientific description of an alien world, compared to our own world so that we may understand it. But the comparison cuts both ways. We begin to see our own world through the alien, and what we see is our pervasive dualism. This scientist/spy reports that if an ambassador is sent openly to Gethen "he must be warned that unless he is very self-assured, or senile, his pride will suffer. A man wants his virility regarded, a woman wants her femininity appreciated however indirect and subtle the indications of regard and appreciation. On Winter they will not exist. One is respected and judged only as a human being. It is an appalling experience" (p. 69)

In those words one hears the accents of utopian novelists since Thomas More. The trick that More perfected, using "Nowhere" to get a hold on the iniquities of his own world, has been adapted here for modern ends that More, that "man for all seasons" would have understood. But "Winter" is a world of one season, and our attention, in any case, must remain on the way this lack of sexual difference is developed in conformity with the constraints of this "popular" genre, science fiction.

A science fiction novel ought to have a strong story to carry the reader along, though it need not have characters with psychological depth. *The Left Hand of Darkness* goes well beyond the minimum requirements in both story and character. It has political intrigue, an adventure story ending in a chase across the frozen wastes of the planet, and even something like a love story: the story, at any rate, of a relationship of growing intimacy between two characters, reaching a point of climax when all the lines of action are brought together during the chase across the glacier. Once again, however, we must attend only to how the counterfact of androgyny is mapped onto these more purely narrative concerns.

This story focuses on the ambassador from other worlds, a perfectly normal male human being—seen as a "pervert" by the Gethenians because he is always "in kemmer"—who must seek to understand his hosts and win them over to a political alliance. This political mission is complicated enormously by his difficulty in relating to the androgynous Gethenians—and theirs in accepting him. As he puts it himself early in the novel, "I was still far from being able to see the people of the planet through their own eyes. I tried to, but my efforts took the form of self-consciously seeing a Gethenian first as a man, then as a woman, forcing him into those categories so irrelevant to his nature and so essential to my own" (p. 9).

Within the political story, his inability to "read" the Gethenians makes the ambassador unable to distinguish friend from foe—with disastrous consequences. Within the story of personal relationship, this same inability prevents him from accepting the reality of his alien friend until, again, it is too late or almost so:

> And I saw then again, and for good, what I had always been afraid to see and had pretended not to see in him: that he was a woman as well as a man. Any need to explain the sources of that fear vanished with the fear; what I was left with was, at last, acceptance of him as he was. Until then I had rejected him, refused him his own reality. He had been quite right to say that he, the only person on Gethen who trusted me was the only Gethenian I distrusted. For he was the only one who had entirely accepted me as a human being; who had liked me personally and given me entire personal loyalty: and who therefore had demanded of me an equal degree of recognition, of acceptance. I had not been willing to give it. I had been afraid to give it. I had not wanted to give my trust, my friendship to a man who was a woman, a woman who was a man. [pp. 177–178]

As is so often the case, the most important moment in this science fiction novel is the moment of confrontation with the alien. LeGuin's novel uses this standard element of the genre, but in a most unusual way. In a whole world of aliens, it is only one who is confronted, and the confrontation comes not on the first encounter but almost at the last. Finally, the alien who is confronted is not different in any way from "normal" human beings. In the tent on the glacier the ambassador's companion enters kemmer and, because of the ambassador's male presence, enters it as a potential mate for him. It would take only a touch for this process to complete itself, and for the male ambassador to share a sexual embrace with a female of his own species, a person whom he has come to love. The real confrontation is here. The alien is a woman—but a woman who is more than a woman. Knowing that a touch would inevitably lead to sexual intimacy, they do not touch. As the ambassador records it, "For us to meet sexually would be for us to meet once more as aliens. We had touched in the only way we could touch. We left it at that. I do not know if we were right" (p. 178).

Much of the power of this book comes from the way that the difference between the sexes and the difference between human and alien are inscribed in the same space. And they are inscribed by a linguistic difference that also inhabits this same space, for this is the space of differance itself. The ambassador who narrates most of the story is continually stumbling over the way that sexual difference has been inscribed in language. Referring to a fellow spectator at the ceremony opening the novel he calls him a "man"—and then mutters, "*man* I must say, having said *he* and *his*" (p. 4), but this system of sexual difference goes deeper than grammar, as he is intermittently aware. Sometimes he damns the "effeminate deviousness" of his hosts or curses himself for "missing another signal" (p. 10). At a crucial conference he is so wrapped up in his own communicative problems that he cannot believe that his host believes him: " 'I believe you,' said the stranger, the alien alone with me, and so strong had my access of self-alienation been that I looked up at him bewildered." His host, whom he later comes to know and love, tries to educate him in the politics of that world, defining patriotism for him: " 'No, I don't mean love, when I say patriotism. I mean fear. The fear of the other' " (p. 13)—and thus is the theme of difference introduced.

The problem of a suitable pronoun for the androgynes has troubled not only the narrator but the author as well. As she observed on one occasion,

> Many feminists have been grieved or aggrieved by *The Left Hand of Darkness* because the androgynes in it are called "he" throughout. In the third person singular, the English generic pronoun is the same as the masculine pronoun. A fact worth reflecting upon. And it's a trap, with no way out, because the exclusion of the feminine (she) and the neuter (it) from the generic/masculine (he) makes the use of either of them more specific, more unjust, as it were, than the use of "he." [*The Wind's Twelve Quarters*, p. 93]

The problem could not be solved in *The Left Hand of Darkness*, only foregrounded, laid bare. But LeGuin solved it in an illuminating way on another occasion. She took her early story, "Winter's King," written before she knew the Gethenians were androgynous, and she rewrote it for a second publication, keeping such masculine titles as King and Lord but changing the pronouns to she and her. The effect is staggering: precisely like a sex change in a person you know. The whole world reorients itself around a few pronouns. Imagine retelling the life of Joan of Arc as the story of John of Arc, with masculine pronouns. There's differance, for you, and there's power, the power of difference and language. What we don't have, of course, is a way of telling a story about a person who is neither a man nor a woman.

Within *The Left Hand of Darkness* itself, the constellation of language, difference, and fear is developed extensively, in a manner that can be illuminated by posing it against two other texts that are concerned with this same constellation: the *Essay on the Origin of Languages* of Jean-Jacques Rousseau and the commentary on that text in Jacques Derrida's *Of Grammatology*;[4] for it is Rousseau who connects the nature of language with the alien encounter, and Derrida who reminds us that this is the case:

> Upon meeting others, a savage man will initially be frightened. Because of his fears he sees the others as bigger and stronger

than himself. He calls them *giants*. After many experiences he recognizes that these so-called giants are neither bigger nor stronger than he. Their stature does not approach the idea he had initially attached to the word giant. So he invents another name common to them and to him, such as the name *man*, for example, and leaves *giant* to the false object that had impressed him during his illusion. That is how the figurative word is born before the literal word, when our gaze is held in passionate fascination; and how it is that the first idea it conveys to us is not that of the truth. [Rousseau, quoted in *Of Grammatology*, p. 276]

Does the example of fear come by chance? Does not the metaphoric origin of language lead us necessarily to a situation of threat, distress, and dereliction, to an archaic solitude, to the anguish of dispersion? Absolute fear would then be the first encounter of the other as other: as other than I and as other than itself. I can answer the threat of the other as other (than I) only by transforming it into another (than itself), through altering it in my imagination, my fear, or my desire. [Derrida, *Of Grammatology*, p. 277]

Rousseau is simply giving an example of the way that figurative meaning precedes literal meaning in his version of the origin of language. But his example—emerging from what depth of intuitive insight?—is that of an alien encounter. "Does the example of fear come by chance?" asks Derrida. And to that I would add that the object of that fear—the giant, the monster, the alien—does not come by chance, either. As Derrida glosses Rousseau's fable, the threat posed by the other is dealt with grammatologically, by inscribing the other in a discourse, calling him a "giant," displacing him from himself. The violence of language is a *domesticating* violence. It alienates in order to tame.

The situation presented by LeGuin in the confrontation we have been examining is both like and unlike that described by Rousseau. Certainly the fear of the alien is present in both cases, and the relationship of this fear to language is central in both. In

THE LEFT HAND OF DIFFERENCE

Rousseau's case the name "giant" is seen as a response by language to the otherness of the other—a response which Derrida describes as a further alienation. But in LeGuin's case it is language which creates the alienation in the first place. Because there is no alternative to he and she in English, there is no way to domesticate an androgyne in language. And the language, it is clear, is homologous to the culture and the consciousness of those who use it.

In the classificatory systems that dominated Western thought from the Old Testament through the Renaissance, there was no space between the categories of male and female. Male and female created He them—and they stayed that way. Though Plato and his followers were interested in the androgyne as a unified ideal of humanity, the largely Aristotelean science of the Renaissance classified actual hermaphrodites as monsters. Caught in a binary opposition between natural and unnatural, naturally born beings of androgynous composition were simply classified as unnatural monstrosities (MacLean, *The Renaissance Notion of Woman*, p. 39). LeGuin has taken special pains to prevent her aliens from being perceived as either super- or sub-human. They are mainly ordinary human beings who happen to be neuter most of the time and then either male or female as chance will have it. With respect to our system of classification, they represent pure difference, or "differance." They are perpetually different from themselves, a deferred difference, since they can expect to be he, she, and it but will never rest permanently in any prononimal category. They are not monsters, nor Platonic ideas; they are just outside our categories, calling them into question.

In considering Rousseau's linking of fear to mis-naming, Derrida comments that for Rousseau fear is "the first passion," and pity its proper antidote. He then follows Rousseau down a curious byway, noting that for Rousseau pity is a "spontaneous movement . . . toward everything living, whatever may be its species and sex." Rousseauian pity, according to Derrida, recognizes no differences. It is opposed to love, the "amorous passion" that introduces possessiveness, jealousy, preference, "that is to say, difference," into human existence. Rousseau attributes this corruption of a pure emotion to femininity, an "arresting of nature by woman." Derrida thus brings out the patriarchal and invidious use of difference by Rousseau, quoting him as calling love "a factitious sentiment, born of social usage, super-subtly celebrated by women, with care for the establishment of their empire, and rendering dominant the sex that ought to obey."

LeGuin, on the other hand, examining this same ground of alienation, language, and passion, presents a notion of love that is anything but a possessive move in a game of dominance. For her it is fear, rooted in patriotism, that is the possessive, chauvinistic passion, while love is that which refuses possession, for it requires and maintains difference in order to exist. One instance of this is chronicled by the ambassador, who tells us what happened when his companion entered kemmer as a potential woman. The sexual tension between the two companions, "admitted now and understood, but not assuaged" led to a great "assurance of friendship," so strong that "it might as well be called, now as later, love" (p. 179). This is a strange avowal of passion but then it is a strange passion, or perhaps a passion for strangeness, for he goes on to say in the next sentence, "But it was from the difference between us, not from the affinities and likenesses, but from the difference, that that love came: and it was itself the bridge, the only bridge, across what divided us (p. 178).

To build a bridge across difference does not sound exactly like deconstruction, but it is by no means the opposite of it. It is also LeGuin's habitual mode of dealing with invidious binary oppositions. If you can recall that Pythagorean list we glanced at earlier, several of those oppositions are interwoven in the title and major concerns of LeGuin's novel.

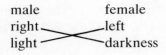

In reading the book we discover that its title is a fragment of a Gethenian poem that includes the phrase, "Light is the left hand of darkness / and darkness is the right hand of light." In the Pythagorean formula, light is linked vertically with right (and male). In the poem, however, light is linked with left and darkness with right. The pairings are intertwined. LeGuin has woven a text across the binary gap. This is her way. We could emulate this by saying that "male is the left hand of female," but LeGuin does not insist on this. She does, however, attend to other binary oppositions.

In their journey across the glacier the man and his androgynous companion find that fear sometimes saves them from disastrous missteps and that when there are no shadows cast by the hazy sky they are lost in light. As the androgyne puts it, " 'Fear's very useful. Like darkness; like shadow. . . . It's queer that daylight's not enough. We need the shadows, in order to walk.' " To which the other replies: " 'Light, dark. Fear, courage. Cold, warmth. Female, male. It is yourself, Therem. Both in one. A shadow on snow' " (pp. 190–91). Not one as opposed to the other, but both in one.

The whole movement of LeGuin's novel is toward a final moment in which the androgynous child of the ambassador's beloved friend asks the ambassador about his dead parent—and more. The child stammers: "Will you tell us how he died?—Will you tell us about the other worlds out among the stars—the other kinds of men, the other lives" (p. 215). These are the last words of the novel, a request for a story about aliens: "tell us about . . . the other." Even here the ambassador's language, which is LeGuin's language (together they are an androgyne) betrays its subject: tell us how *he* died, tell us about *men*; but by now in this book such words are half erased, with an imaginary Derridean cross written through them. We have encountered enough phrases like "My landlady, a voluble man" (p. 35) and "the King was pregnant" (p. 72) to be wary of the whole verbal enterprise. That there is no pronoun for a human being as such, for a person, is now our problem as well as LeGuin's. And that has been the point.

But I do violence to LeGuin's undertaking if I seem to suggest that this whole many-faceted text (most of which I have in fact ignored for my purposes here) can be reduced to a single point. The book ends with a request for stories about aliens, which if answered could only result in the domestication of difference in narrative space. But the request is not answered, nor is LeGuin's book itself the answer to this request, for the aliens the young androgyne wants to hear about are ourselves. We are the other lives, "out among the stars." When science fiction really works it does not domesticate the alien but alienates the domestic. It takes us on journeys where we meet the alien and find that he is us. If LeGuin is right, it is only after such a voyage of alienation that we might hope to be reconciled to our own humanity. Seeing ourselves as aliens we may learn to love what is different in ourselves—for the left hand of difference is love.

8

IS THERE A FISH IN THIS TEXT?

> As before, the Pequod steeply leaned over towards the sperm whale's head, now by the counterpoise of both heads, she regained her even keel; though sorely strained you may believe. So, when on one side you hoist in Locke's head, you go over that way; but now, on the other side, hoist in Kant's and you come back again; but in very poor plight. Thus, some minds for ever keep trimming boat. Oh, ye foolish! throw all these thunderheads overboard, and then you will float light and right.
>
> Herman Melville,
> *Moby-Dick*

Contrary to Ishmael's good advice, we have been pulling and hauling at those "thunderheads" for several chapters, not without strain. Time now to tackle smaller fry and let our world shrink to the compass of a classroom once again. The issues are the same—reference and difference—but the problem is to be conceived anew, in terms of the English teacher's most fundamental concern, the teaching of writing. Can we—should we—engage our students in the practice of putting *things* into words? Is it possible for any text to catch a fish? Is it even possible to catch a text?

Let us begin with two fish stories that are not just fish stories but parables about the relationship between words and things.

The first is taken from Ezra Pound's *ABC of Reading*, the second from John Steinbeck's written text for the *Sea of Cortez*.[1]

No man is equipped for modern thinking until he has understood the anecdote of Agassiz and the fish:

A post-graduate student equipped with honours and diplomas went to Agassiz to receive the final and finishing touches. The great man offered him a small fish and told him to describe it.

Post-Graduate Student: 'That's only a sunfish.'

Agassiz: 'I know that. Write a description of it.'

After a few minutes the student returned with the description of the Icthus Heliodiplodokus,or whatever term is used to conceal the common sunfish from vulgar knowledge, family of Heliichthinkerus, etc., as found in textbooks of the subject.

Agassiz again told the student to describe the fish.

The student produced a four-page essay. Agassiz then told him to look at the fish. At the end of three weeks the fish was in an advanced state of decomposition, but the student knew something about it. [*ABC*, pp. 17–18]

The Mexican sierra has "XVII–15–IX" spines in the dorsal fin. These can easily be counted. But if the sierra strikes hard on the line so that our hands are burned, if the fish sounds and nearly escapes and finally comes in over the rail, his colors pulsing and his tail beating the air, a whole new relational externality has come into being—an entity which is more than the sum of the fish plus the fisherman. The only way to count the spines of the sierra unaffected by this second relational reality is to sit in a laboratory, open an evil-smelling jar, remove a stiff colorless fish from formalin solution, count the spines, and write the truth "D.XVII–15–IX." There you have recorded a reality which cannot be assailed—probably the least important reality concerning either the fish or yourself.

It is good to know what you are doing. The man with his pickled fish has set down one truth and has recorded in his experience many lies. The fish is not that color, that texture, that dead, nor does he smell that way. [*Sea*, pp. 2–3]

We can read the Steinbeck as a critique of the Pound, and much of what I have to say here is simply an amplification of that critique. But the criticism I have in mind is not really directed at Pound himself. He is simply the bait for bigger game. I am after a whole methodology in the teaching of reading and writing in America that is based upon the model of Agassiz and the fish, and the imagistic notion of composition that lies behind it. As a composition teacher—a role he assumes frequently in the *ABC of Reading*—Pound suggests such exercises as the following:

1 Let the pupil write the description of a tree.

2 Of a tree without mentioning the name of the tree (larch, pine, etc.) so that the reader will not mistake it for the description of some other kind of tree. [*ABC*, p. 66]

This is Pound's own extension of the Agassiz method to composition. It is a system that privileges the eye, the gaze, and assumes the power of an innocent eye: no names, no studying, no learning—the eye engendering the word. In a word: imagism.

In Pound's "anecdote of Agassiz and the fish," it is strongly suggested that we learn by looking at things. Above all, the student is held to have learned about the fish by repeatedly gazing at it. The student looks and writes, looks and writes, until he sees the fish well and truly—as Pound's disciple Hemingway might have said—and can describe it as it really is. But, using Hemingway's disciple Steinbeck's perspective, we may ask if he knows the fish as a fisherman might know the fish. He knows something about a dead and decomposing creature, but he does not know and cannot (in Roland Barthes's phrase) "speak the fish." He can, however, now speak and write Agassizese, for this is what he has really learned: to produce the sort of writing his teacher wants.

It is a parable of all schoolrooms, is it not, and perhaps a parody of them as well. The student seems to be learning about the subject, but what he is truly learning is to give the teacher what he wants. He seems to be reporting about a real and solid world in a perfectly transparent language, but actually he is learning how to produce a specific kind of discourse, controlled by a particular scientific paradigm, which requires him to be constituted as the subject of that discourse in a particular way and to speak through that discourse of a world made visible by the same controlling paradigm. The teacher's power over the student is plain in Pound's example, and the student's ritual suffering as he endures the smell of the decomposing fish and the embarrassment of the teacher's rebuffs is part of an initiation process he must undergo to enter a scientific community. As Michel Foucault puts it: "First question: who is speaking?"

> Who, among the totality of speaking individuals, is accorded the right to use this sort of language? Who is qualified to do so? Who derives from it his own special quality, his prestige, and from whom, in return, does he receive if not the assurance, at least the presumption that what he says is true? What is the status of the individuals who—alone—have the right, sanctioned by law or tradition, juridically defined or spontaneously accepted, to proffer such a discourse? [*Archaeology of Knowledge*, p. 50][2]

To have the right to speak as a biologist or naturalist, Agassiz's student must be indoctrinated in a set of discursive procedures. To "speak the fish" as a biologist or a fisherman or a poet is to speak in a particular discourse. But we English teachers have been slow to acknowledge this.

The entire edifice of American instruction in written composition rests on a set of assumptions much like Ezra Pound's. We have all been brought up as imagists. We assume that a complete self confronts a solid world, perceiving it directly and accurately, always capable of capturing it perfectly in a transparent language. Bring 'em back alive; just give us the facts, ma'am; the way it was; tell it like it is; and that's the way it is. Perhaps some of our difficulty in teaching composition results from our operating uncritically on this set of assumptions—all of which have been questioned so thoroughly, now, that the whole naive epistemology upon which they rest is lying in ruins around us. In response to this situation, we can assume that our practice has nothing to do with theory, or we can make the opposite assumption and try to use the new developments in structuralist and post-structuralist theory as the basis for a new practice in the teaching of composition. Many will choose the former of these two assumptions, and perhaps they will be right to do so, for it will not be easy to found an American practice upon these largely European theories. Nevertheless, that is what I would urge upon my fellow teachers of reading and writing.

To make the case for such a project, and in so doing to take a few steps in the direction of a more fully developed semiotics of composition, will be my object in the remainder of this discussion. My method will be to apply a semiotic procedure of analysis to Pound's parable of instruction, returning, like the student of Agassiz, to this specimen again and again until it stinks in all our nostrils. Like the student in the parable, we shall have to learn to "see" our object. Pound's anecdote comes to us in the form of a text. To see it with some degree of thoroughness, then, we must see it "transtextually" (in Gérard Genette's terminology), as a text related to other texts. First we shall work backward from Pound toward the texts that he has adapted in creating his own, and then outward to some other texts by and around Agassiz, concluding with some texts related mainly by their own concern to speak, in some way, the fish.

The anecdote of Agassiz, the student, and the fish might have come to Pound in any number of ways, written and oral, but there are two versions available to us in print, which were also available to Pound before he wrote the *ABC of Reading* in 1934. They are Nathaniel Southgate Shaler's recollection of his initiation into Agassiz's world in 1859, as recorded in *The Autobiography of Nathaniel Southgate Shaler* (1907), and Samuel H. Scudder's recollection of his very similar experience at about the same time, first published in *Every Saturday* magazine in 1874.

Both of these versions of two very similar experiences were extracted from their original texts by an English professor at Cornell University, Lane Cooper, and published in 1917 in a little volume called *Louis Agassiz as a Teacher: Illustrative Extracts on His Method of Instruction*.[3] There is a strong presumption that Pound in fact knew Cooper's little volume and drew his anecdote from it. I say that the presumption is strong, because it is Cooper who draws the parallel between biology and the study of poetry, between the natural scientist and the English teacher. As he puts it in his preface, the reason why an English teacher should be moved to issue a book on Agassiz is that "I have been taught, and I try to teach others, after a method in essence identical with that employed by the great naturalist" (p. v).

In his "Introductory Note" Cooper develops this theme further:

> Within recent years we have witnessed an extraordinary development in certain studies, which, though superficially different from those pursued by Agassiz, have an underlying bond of unity with them, but which are generally carried on without reference to principles governing the investigation of every organism and all organic life. I have in mind, particularly, the spread of literary and linguistic study in America during the last few decades, and the lack of a common standard of judgment among those who engage in such study. Most persons do not, in fact, discern the close, though not obvious, relation between investigation in biology or zoology and the observation and comparison of those organic forms which we call forms of literature and works of art. Yet the notion that a poem or a speech should possess the organic structure, as it were, of a living creature is basic in the thought of the great literary critics of all time. . . . We study a poem, the work of man's art, in the same way that Agassiz made Shaler study a fish, the work of God's art; the object in either case, is to discover the relation between form or structure and function or essential effect. [*Agassiz as Teacher*, pp. 2–4]

Forty years later, when Northrop Frye suggested that the study of literature be made more like the study of biology, this came as a great shock, even at Cornell University, where I happened to be studying at the time, and where Lane Cooper's memory was still green. The shock, I submit, was not so much in the suggestion that literary study learn from science, as in the different notion of biology put forward by Frye:

> As long as biology thought of animal and vegetable forms of life as constituting its subject, the different branches of biology were largely efforts of cataloguing. As soon as it was the existence of forms of life themselves that had to be explained, the theory of evolution and the concepts of protoplasm and the cell poured into biology and completely revitalized it.
>
> It occurs to me that literary criticism is now in such a state of naive induction as we find in a primitive science. [*Anatomy of Criticism*, p. 15][4]

Frye drew a careful parallel between biology and literary study, arguing that biology became a full-fledged science when it went beyond close observation of the individual object to study the systems by which individual objects were in fact ordered and perceived. Frye was attempting in his own way (as Geoffrey Hartman noticed long ago) to move toward a structuralism in literary study. It was this that made his work so startling and refreshing at the time, and it was this that prepared those Anglo-American critics influenced by Frye to receive structuralism hospitably when it began to be exported from the continent of Europe.

The shift in literary studies indicated through the different uses of the biological analogy by Lane Cooper in 1917 and Northrop Frye in 1957 is only part of the history we are considering. The scientific metaphor itself conceals something in the agendas of both Cooper and Frye that must also be considered, and in the case of Cooper this is especially important. Stripped of its scientific cloak, what precisely was the method of literary study that Cooper was advocating back in 1917?

Cooper offered a method that was essentially hermeneutic: "we study a poem, the work of man's art, in the same way that Agassiz made Shaler study a fish, the work of God's art." The appearance of God in this equation is no accident but part of its design. Substitute a tree for the fish and Joyce Kilmer's infamous poem can be generated by a simple, almost mathematical operation: "Poems are made by fools like me, / But only God can make a tree." And who makes the fools, one wishes to ask? This excessive anthropomorphizing of the creative principle in the universe is a major problem in Western theology, but it is a kind of red herring in the present discourse and we must abandon it. For our purposes, what is important in Cooper's formulation is its focus on the single object, fish or text, the meaning of which is guaranteed not by its place in an order or system, but by the creator whose creature it is and whose presence in the object is signified by the object's structure. Before fish or poem, we are in the presence of presence, of metaphysical presence, that is, which guarantees the object's meaning. As Cooper himself observes, "Agassiz, considered in his philosophical relations, was a Platonist, since he clearly believed that the forms of nature expressed the essential ideas of a divine intelligence" (p. 3).

There is more to Pound's fish than meets the eye. He has suppressed the Platonism of his model, of course, but his procedure should make us wonder how much latent Platonism there may be in all attempts to see the object as in itself it really is, whether the object be a tree, a fish, or a text. For here is the point at which the older criticism and pedagogy are confronted most directly by semiotic theory and practice. Is the object's meaning guaranteed by reference to its creator's intention in making it, or is its meaning a function of its position in a system of objects linked to it by paradigmatic and syntagmatic processes? Taking Pound's anecdote of the fish as our object, I wish to argue that we can interpret it best only by taking our eyes off it, denying it status as a thing in itself, and reading it as intertextually as we can within the limits of the present discourse.

We can begin by looking at the actual pre-texts that lie behind Pound's text. In considering them, we will see what Pound retained, what he suppressed, what he added, and what he transformed for his own purposes. Before receiving his fish,

Nathaniel Shaler was given a preliminary oral examination, which revealed that he knew some Latin and Greek, some French and a good deal of German. It was also determined that he had read Agassiz's *Essay on Classification* and "had noted in it the influence of Schelling's views" (Cooper, *Louis Agassiz*, p. 19). The exam ended with a fencing match (quite a literal one, with masks and foils in play). Only after all this came the famous fish:

> When I sat me down before my tin pan, Agassiz brought me a small fish, placing it before me with the rather stern require-ment that I should study it, but should on no account talk to anyone concerning it, nor read anything related to fishes, until I had his permission so to do. [p. 22]

For a week Agassiz refused to hear a report on the fish. As Shaler tells us, "At first this neglect was distressing; but I saw that it was a game, for he was, as I discerned rather than saw, covertly watching me" (p. 22). Shaler looks, Agassiz watches him looking, and Shaler discerns rather than sees Agassiz watch-ing him looking. Gazes run rampant here. At the end of the week Shaler made a one hour oral report, to which he received the response, "That is not right." Recognizing that "he was playing a game with me to see if I were capable of doing hard, continuous work without the support of a teacher," Shaler went to work for another week and at last satisfied Agassiz. "The incident of the fish," he writes, "made an end of my novitiate" (p. 25).

At this point I wish to draw a few of the conclusions that the juxtaposition of Shaler's and Pound's versions of the fish inci-dent makes available to us. First, it was obvious to Shaler that he was involved in a power game, a ritual, a novitiate. Second, the rules of the game—no reading up on the subject, strict concen-tration on the single object—are remarkably like the techniques developed by I. A. Richards and the New Critics for the teaching of poetry. Third, the candidate, having read his teacher's essay on classification before being given his object for analysis, is

remarkably *un*like the untutored undergraduate confronting a
poem or the freshman composition student told to describe a
tree. Fourth, in this version of the fish story, the fish itself is not
named, nor is there any *writing* about the fish beyond the taking
of notes. The reports to Agassiz are made orally, not in the form
of written compositions as they are in Pound's anecdote. Now let
us look at Scudder's report on his very similar experience.

Scudder, who wanted to study nice clean insects, was nevertheless given a fish, a *haemulon*, to study. Scudder makes much
of the fish's disagreeable smell, its "ghastly" and "hideous"
appearance, and the limitations under which he worked: "I
might not use a magnifying-glass; instruments of all kinds were
interdicted" (Cooper, *Louis Agassiz*, p. 43). At last, he got the
idea of drawing the fish, and began to see features in it he had not
noticed before. For this he was rewarded by Agassiz, who told
him, "That is right, a pencil is one of the best of eyes" (p. 43).
But, when questioned, he did not satisfy the master. He was told
he hadn't seen "one of the most conspicuous features of the
animal, which is as plainly before your eyes as the fish itself; look
again, look again!" and, as Scudder tells us, he was then left to
his "misery." When he hadn't found the missing "conspicuous
feature" by the end of the afternoon of his second day with the
fish he was told to go home and report in the morning for an
examination *without looking at the fish*. He says that he walked
home, spent a wakeful night, and returned in the morning to face
"a man who seemed to be quite as anxious as I that I should see
for myself what he saw. 'Do you perhaps mean,' I asked, 'that
the fish has symmetrical sides with paired organs?'" To which
the "thoroughly pleased Professor Agassiz" replied, "of course!
of course!" (p. 45).

From this version, too, some conclusions may be drawn.
This has less the air of an initiation than Shaler's experience and
more that of a puzzle or riddle: guess what the professor has in
mind! Here, too, the examination is oral, not written. It is Pound
who has brought writing into his exemplary fable. Seeing is
emphasized here, too, but the final problem is not exactly a

problem in vision. Scudder is in fact told to solve the problem without looking at the fish. And solve it he does. But bilateral symmetry is a feature of a classification system rather than a simple fact of nature. It cannot be "seen" apart from the concept that gives it status, and it certainly cannot be drawn easily in the case of fish, since their flat shape leads us normally to draw either one side of a fish or the other. Scudder's anecdote would seem, then, to illustrate superbly the principle that vision is always mediated, that the concept enables the perception. "Seeing" itself is not a simple function but a complex one, and scientific seeing is always dependent upon instruments. If not the microscope, then the pencil; if not the pencil, then the conceptual system, which is itself, of course, an instrument, an apparatus that enables a certain sort of vision. Shaler had read Agassiz's *Essay on Classification* before he was given *his* fish. It is, by the way, an essay on the classification of fish, not simply on classification in general. And what of Scudder? What did he do during his sleepless night? Did he just lie there thinking of fish? Or did he talk to anyone about them? Might he have consulted Agassiz's own essay on the classification of fishes? Whence came his miraculous vision of a fish with "symmetrical sides and paired organs"? What organs did he "see" and how did he see them? He does not tell us.

Pound, of course, tells us more. Let us return to him like a good student to his ghastly fish and examine him yet another time, for as he says himself, "The proper METHOD for studying poetry and good letters is the method of contemporary biologists, that is careful first-hand examination of the matter, and continual COMPARISON of one 'slide' or specimen with another" (*ABC*, p. 17). Pound presents the anecdote to us *as* an anecdote, which allows him a raconteur's license to improve his material, and improve it he does, for he is a superb raconteur and a well-schooled rhetorician. First he gives us an arresting generalization: "No man . . ."; then he introduces an alazon in the form of a *discipulus gloriosus* with "honors and diplomas" seeking "final and finishing touches." Agassiz, a "great" man, is

our *eiron*, offering a small fish to the proud student, who remarks in his pridefulness, "That's *only* a sunfish." Only! He will
rue that only, will he not? The student returns in a matter of
minutes with a textbook description of a fish with a Latin name.
Here Pound, who often had no quarrel with either learning or
Latin, makes fun of the name as obfuscatory. He associates the
student, not the teacher, with this name by an intricate metonymy that includes a partial homonymity between the student's
*diplo*mas and the name Helio*diplo*dokus. We may speculate that
Pound vaguely remembered Scudder's *haemulon* in inventing
the Heliodiplodokus, but he is merely having fun. One could
have had fun with Scudder's original fish, too, for the *haemulon*
is better known as the "grunt," because of the noise it makes
when taken out of the water. But how could a student of Agassiz
ever learn about the reason for the common name by simply
examining a dead fish? It does not grunt when removed from the
alcohol bottle. We are back to the question of what it means to
know the fish, but Pound is our fish for the moment and we must
continue to play him.

Pound's student next produces a four-page essay, perhaps
because of Pound's interest in writing, perhaps simply as a way
of making his efforts concrete. Pound's fish decomposes badly,
while Shaler's and Scudder's do not, because they keep them wet
and replace them in their alcohol bottles every night like good
little students, but it certainly makes a fine story this way, a far
better story than those of Scudder and Shaler themselves.
Pound's student suffers these indignities for three weeks, Shaler
for two, and Scudder for only three days. Pound's exaggeration
improves the tale, of course, and is of the essence of the anec-
dotal mode. One suspects, however, that Shaler has "improved"
his material in this respect, too; that for him Scudder is a pretext. The story grows in each retelling, like many fish stories. But
what should we, looking at Pound looking at Agassiz looking at
Shaler looking at Scudder, looking at their fish, learn from all
this?

We may ask ourselves what is the reality, the truth behind

the incident, but we will find no ready answer. Pound's distortions are clear enough, but what is he distorting? Shaler, boxer and fencer, gives us an initiation ritual. Scudder, the fastidious entomologist, gives us a puzzle. Both students pass their tests and go on to become professors themselves. What we see is a stage in their learning a discourse (as Foucault puts it) or acquiring a paradigm (in Thomas S. Kuhn's terminology). Pound, the imagist, gives us a recipe for imagism: look at the object and write about the way it looks without naming it and you will capture its truth. Each one sees what his own discourse lets him see. And what do we see? Why, the truth, of course.

"What *is Truth*; said jesting *Pilate*; And would not stay for an Answer"—so grumbles the father of British empiricism, Francis Bacon, in the opening sentence of his *Essayes*, but those who stay with Bacon himself to learn what truth is may not be satisfied. Observing in passing that poets lie for pleasure's sake, Bacon goes on to tell us that "This same *Truth*, is a Naked, and Open day light, that doth not shew, the Masques and Mummeries, and Triumphs of the world, halfe so stately, and daintily, as Candle-lights." In short, Bacon himself can answer Pilate's question with nothing better than a metaphor—Truth is a Naked and Open day light—as if he were himself a lying poet whose language could not find a naked and open way of saying what truth is. The question is answered in a more satisfying (more truthful?) way by one more comfortable in a jester's cap and bells than Pontius Pilate:

> What is truth? A moving army of metaphors, metonymies and anthropomorphisms, in short a summa of human relationships that are being poetically and rhetorically sublimated, transposed, and beautified until after long and repeated use, a people considers them as solid, canonical, and unavoidable. Truths are illusions whose illusionary nature has been forgotten. [Friedrich Nietzsche, "On Truth and Lies"]

To tell the truth, to capture reality in writing, is a noble aim, and to teach such skill were to make instruction in composition a high calling indeed. But such work is not easy. I propose to consider some of the difficulties by taking an example or two from Agassiz, since he has been put before us by Pound and Cooper as an exemplar of both instruction and accurate perception. Confronted with a new phenomenon in his own experience, how did he perceive it; in what terms did he write about such a thing himself?

In 1846, Agassiz visited Philadelphia, where we are told he encountered black Americans for the first time. His biographer, Edward Lurie, has given us a brief extract from a letter he wrote to his mother upon that occasion:

> I hardly dare to tell you the painful impression I received, so much are the feelings they gave me contrary to all our ideas of the brotherhood of man and unique origin of our species. But truth before all. The more pity I felt at the sight of this degraded and degenerate race the more . . . impossible it becomes for me to repress the feeling that they are not of the same blood we are. [*Louis Agassiz*, p. 257][5]

In public essays, he repeated the same themes, arguing that blacks were by nature submissive, obsequious, and imitative, and that "white relations with colored people would be conducted more intelligently if the fundamental differences between human types were realized and understood" (Lurie's summary, pp. 260, 262).

"Many an eye / He trained to Truth's exact severity," said the poet Lowell in his encomiastic verses upon the great man. And "Truth before all," said Agassiz to his mother, but what is truth? What did Agassiz *see* when he looked at black Americans? What he saw was surely not an unmediated vision. It was, in fact, what many other "cultivated" individuals of his time saw, but he was not an ordinary individual. He was a scientist, a zoologist, and his views carried weight. He developed a theory of humanity, asserting that there were eight distinct types—Caucasian, Arctic, Mongol, American Indian, Negro, Hottentot, Malayan, and Australian—insisting that these types were distinct in origin, with "their differences," as Lurie puts it, "stamped on them from the beginning." In the decade leading up to the Civil War, these views were of more than passing interest. His biographer, in fact, comes to the following melancholy conclusion: "within ten years Agassiz had provided racial supremacists with primary arguments. . . . That Agassiz permitted his reputation to support doctrines of social and racial inequality was indeed tragic" (Lurie, p. 265).

Truth before all, said Agassiz, but what is truth? For Agassiz, truth had, as Lane Cooper pointed out, a very Platonic cast. This emerges clearly in his response to Darwin's work, where his refusal to accept the theory of evolution gradually undermined his standing as a scientist. He became a forerunner of our contemporary "creation scientists," in fact, and did everything he could to reconcile scientific findings with received religious truths. In the *Essay on Classification* itself, he had argued that reality was regularly found to agree with *a priori* conceptions of it, which, he maintained, demonstrated that the human and the Divine intellects were linked by "an identity of operations" (see Lurie, p. 283). This view led him to assert that all species were absolute, fixed from their creation, and hence to reject all fossil evidence for evolution. There were no variants from species, he claimed, asserting at a meeting of the Boston Society for Natural History that "in 6,000 fishes, he had not seen a variety" (Lurie, p. 297).

We are back to looking at fish again, but on a grander scale, and we must ask a question: why couldn't Agassiz *see* the evidence in fish and fossils that many other scientists of his time saw in them. The answer, as Thomas Kuhn elaborates it for us in so many passages of *The Structure of Scientific Revolutions*, is that vision depends upon expectations to a considerable degree.[6] Because Agassiz refused to accept the paradigm shift in his discipline, he could not "see" the evidence that might have persuaded him to accept the shift. We "see" and "are" in discourse.

The lesson to be drawn from this example of Agassiz and the

fish is that what the student needs from the teacher is help in seeing discourse structures themselves in all their fullness and their power. The way to see the fish and to write the fish is first to see how one's discourse writes the fish. And the way to see one discourse is to see more than one. To write the fish in many modes is finally to see that one will never catch *the* fish in any one discourse. As teachers of writing we have a special responsibility to help our students gain awareness of discourse structures and the ways in which they both enable and constrain our vision. And the only way to do this is to read and write in a range of discursive modes.

Having made this point, I wish to add a necessary qualification. The existence of specific discursive codes seems to me beyond argument, and their constraining effect on the actual practice of writing is a necessary corollary of their existence; but it would be unwarranted to assume from this that such constraints are absolute and fixed. Codes change. Discursive practice modifies discursive systems, which are never completely closed. In short, there is always room for creativity in any discursive order, but it is attained by mastering the practice of the discourse to a degree that enables new utterances to be formed, which in turn become a part of the body of discursive models and finally effect changes in the code itself.

I would like to conclude by offering an example of creativity at work in what has been widely recognized as one of the most rigid discursive systems ever to operate in English literature: Augustan poetry, with its heroic couplets and poetic diction, so severely criticized by Wordsworth and others as unnatural, artificial, and totally incapable of seeing or writing "the fish," offering us instead such locutions as "finny tribe" and "scaly breed." The indictment is certainly correct, up to a point, but in acknowledging it we should also recognize that there is nothing especially fishy about such scientific statements as Scudder's "symmetrical sides with paired organs." Every discourse is a net that captures some aspects of its objects at the necessary cost of allowing others to slip through. Even "finny tribe" captures something of the reality of fish. But let us look at the actual practice of an Augustan poet. Here is a teenage versifier of some talent working in the pastoral mode. He has, in fact, just committed a "scaly breed" two lines before, but he goes on:

> Our plenteous streams a various race supply,
> The bright-eyed perch with fins of Tyrian dye,
> The silver eel in shining volumes rolled,
> The yellow carp in scales bedropped with gold,
> Swift trouts, diversified with crimson stains,
> And pikes, the tyrants of the watery plains.
>   ["Windsor Forest," ll. 141–146]

This is a decorative art, meant to recall the known rather than reveal the unknown, and not simply to recall it but to clothe it in elegant connotations of art, riches, power, and learning. But, for all that, one would not wish to say that the young Alexander Pope had failed, here, to capture something of the color, movement, and even the behavior of his quarry. His pike, for instance, are well cast as tyrants of the underwater world. He is using an obvious formula—adjective, fish name, prepositional descriptive phrase—and he is taking his colors from a rich and royal palette: gold, silver, crimson, Tyrian (purple), and yellow. But there are some creative strokes, nonetheless, and his "silver eel in shining volumes rolled" manages, as he might have said himself, "to snatch a grace beyond the reach of art."

In short, even as a youthful apprentice, wandering in fancy's maze, he had begun to achieve a mastery of his discourse that enabled him to rewrite its possibilities. He became, of course, a master of English literary history as well as of his own form of discourse. He edited Shakespeare; he knew the works of Chaucer, Spenser, and Milton well; and he had a superb critical eye for the best in his own era. As even Ezra Pound says of Pope (in the *ABC*, p. 170), "He is constantly fishing out the better writers. Sic Dunciad II, 124: Congreve, Addison, and Prior. 127: Gay, sieved out from seven authors now completely forgotten." Pope not only mastered his own poetic discourse; he also cast a wide net and drew upon many other texts to enrich his own.

Among the forty or fifty lines from Pope's work that Pound selects to illustrate his strengths as a poet in the *ABC of Reading* is one couplet that will serve to conclude this attempt to illustrate how what we call "creativity" works to transcend the limits of discursive practice. These lines are taken from Book I of the *Dunciad*. They are part of a speech in which the goddess of Dullness is described as showing to her chosen disciples the proper ways to achieve dullness themselves. One thing she shows them is

> How Index-learning turns no student pale,
> Yet holds the eel of science by the tail:

George Sherburn, whose edition of Pope I used as an under-graduate, found "the eel of science" a "sparklingly trenchant" bit of "verbal marksmanship." I, too, think well of the image, though it seems to me more a matter of constructing something that was not there before than of hitting a pre-existing target. Surely, the eel of science is not a matter of seeing at all. What Pope wanted was an image that would convey something that ought to be a difficult task—the acquisition of learning—the sort of task that might well turn a student pale. He personified the abstraction, Index-learning, as a kind of cheap substitute for real learning, an easy way to fake an actual acquaintance with texts. Holding an eel by the tail came to him as the image of difficulty— but from where did this image swim up into his consciousness? I think it came from the river Thames of "Windsor Forest," his youthful exercise in pastoral verse. The image in "Windsor Forest" of "the shining eel in silver volumes rolled" contains in that word "volumes" the connecting link between the two poems. The word "volume" comes from a Latin word meaning coil, roll, and hence scroll. When parchment scrolls gave way to bound books the word "volume" was extended to rectangular books as well as rolled scrolls. Pope's "shining volumes rolled" is a clever archaism, restoring to the word "volume" its sense of scroll. In "Windsor Forest" some learning attaches to the eel, even as political power attaches to the pike. In *The Dunciad*, the learning rejected by those Index-learners who do not read their volumes is signified by the absence of the volumes in this new image of the eel of science. The eel of science is an eel and not some other kind of fish because only the eel comes in the form of a volume. The eel, of course, is also slippery and hard to hold, but Index-learning, tutored by Dullness, can reduce both the lustre and the slipperiness of those shining volumes, and hold the eel of science by the tail.

I am suggesting that what we are normally content to accept as hidden within the black box called creativity can here be glimpsed as an intertextual process, the suppression of which generates the power of the final image. The startling or surprising aspects of the image of the eel of science in the *Dunciad*—which is to say the unexpectedness that gives it a high level of information and hence much of its poetical quality—is achieved by Pope's erasure of some parts of his train of thought, crudely measurable here by the disappearance or nonappearance of the word "volumes." This train of thought itself is an aspect of Pope's mastery of his discipline, his knowledge of languages, his recollection of pre-texts, in this case one of his own, and his habit of searching for images to give substance to a developing flow of thought.

> Some beauties yet no Precepts can declare,
> For there's a happiness as well as care.
> Music resembles Poetry, in each
> Are nameless graces which no methods teach,
> And which a master-hand alone can reach.
> ["Essay on Criticism," ll. 141−45]

We have been considering the ways in which fish may be said to be in, or not in, texts. But this minnow of a problem may be swallowed up by a larger problem of the same species: the problem of the status of the text itself. Suppose that a real text is as elusive as a real fish, losing its own reality the moment we catch it, becoming simply a version of ourselves. And suppose further that we ourselves are simply creatures already swallowed up by a social leviathan, into whose flesh we are inevitably transmuted. This is the problem we must consider in the next chapter. In its strongest and clearest form it has been argued by, of course, Stanley Fish, who has been lurking in the depths of this text all along.

9

WHO CARES ABOUT THE TEXT?

> She said, "But was it true to the text?"
> "Oh, my dear, who cares about the text?"
>
> P.D. James,
> *The Skull Beneath the Skin*

If it is any satisfaction to lovers of the literal, the lady who expresses such a cavalier attitude toward textual fidelity in the epigraph is in fact expunged from the book of life herself shortly thereafter, bashed to death by a relic from the Victorian period. One is tempted to draw from this sequence of events a cautionary moral—but it would be rash to do so, for the very act of drawing such a moral would raise again the specter of textual validity. What is it that might justify me in my desire to interpret this crime of murder as a punishment for indifference to interpretive fidelity? Or, more to the point, perhaps, on what grounds could such an interpretation be confidently rejected? Why won't the text stand still so that one could indeed be true to it or false to it and know which is which?

One set of answers to these questions has been proposed by Stanley Fish, who says, essentially, that the text won't stand still because there is no such thing as the text, which is only and always a figment of the interpreter's imagination. A result of this is that the interpreter seems to become very important. As Fish puts it: "No longer is the critic the humble servant of texts whose glories exist independently of anything he might do" (*Is*

There a Text in This Class? p. 368).[1] This statement is in fact a
bribe, offered to persuade us that we will profit by adopting
Fish's view. There are two things wrong with it—in addition to
the bribery. First, the power offered to interpreters is illusory,
since, in Fish's view, interpreters themselves are always already
the creatures of larger entities called "interpretive communities." Totally controlled by membership in an interpretive community, the interpreter lacks freedom, power, and responsibility. The interpreter is freed from service to the text only to
become the "humble servant" of his ideological group. The
second thing wrong with the bribe is that it betrays Fish's doubts
about his own theory, according to which we could not even have
understood him on his own terms unless we were already members of his community of interpreters. One of the problems of his
theory, in fact, is that it does not allow for any difference
between understanding and belief.

My intention here is to offer a corrective critique of the
argument made by Fish in *Is There a Text in This Class?* In
particular, I shall attack the notion of "interpretive communities" as vague, inconsistently applied, and unworkable. In the
course of this critique I will also sketch out a notion of the
literary text and its uses. Before going on the offensive, however, I want to say two things about Stanley Fish and his theory
of the text. First, I admire his learning, his ingenuity, and his
consummate rhetorical ability. Second, I think that he is right—
not just persuasive, but right—up to a point.

In particular, he is right to question the status of texts,
pointing out that no text is as simply "there" as we have sometimes assumed it to be. Interpretation *does* enter the reading
process at a very early point. And interpretation is never totally
free but always limited by such prior acquisitions as language,
generic norms, social patterns, and beliefs. For a simple but
fundamental example of this, we have only to look at the Book
of Genesis, chapter i: "And God said, let us make man in our
image" (i, 25). The Hebrew word for "God" in this passage
is *Elohim*, the plural of *El*. One could translate the word as

a plural—"The Gods"—instead of a singular, and the plural would then agree grammatically with the other plurals, "us" and "our," which are in the Hebrew, the Vulgate, and the King James text. Obviously, we cannot introduce "The Gods" without embarrassment for all monotheistic interpreters of the text. So the word in Judeo-Christian communities will not only be translated as singular but read in Hebrew as singular. This will not prevent some interpreters from saying that the plural is really there and that it signifies the Trinity. Sir Thomas Browne, in *Religio Medici*, described it as an instance of the royal "we." Others say that the text bears traces of Mesopotamian polytheism. Still others have argued that this God is androgynous and therefore plural. The point is that to a very real extent one's beliefs will color what one reads. For a monotheist *Elohim* is a singular. What is there, in this instance, depends upon an interpretive stance.

This example will serve to illustrate just how far I am willing to go along with Stanley Fish. I hope it will also serve to indicate where I think we should all part company with him. My view of the interpretive complexities of the passage was based upon its appearance in the King James version and a single reference to the Hebrew text. But suppose I had chosen the modern Anchor version for my text: "Then God said I will make man in my image, after my likeness." There are no plurals in this version, *us* and *our* having been replaced by *I* and *my*. To say the very least, this makes the androgynous and polytheistic interpretations more difficult to sustain. Given this particular text, they can hardly even arise. But the very least is all that needs to be said here, for Fish's position is absolutely extreme on this question. He asserts, over and over again, that texts have no properties of their own, that they are always and only what their readers make of them: "Interpretation is not the art of construing but the art of constructing. Interpreters do not decode poems; they make them" (p. 327).

Even this might be acceptable if Fish would admit that making a poem from a text is a different activity from making a text in the first place. The issue here is the extent to which a text may be said to guide or offer resistance to the things one makes of it, whether we call these products poems, works, or interpretations. If we think of printed texts only, for the moment, that come to us in the form of inked shapes on pages, is there any significant difference between a page of *Paradise Lost* and a Rorschach blot? At this point one could introduce a straw Fish to answer that question in the negative. But let me instead make the best possible answer that one could make, holding Fish's stated views in this matter.

This answer would say that, yes, there is a difference but it is not in the texts; it is in the ways we interpret them. I can imagine an interpreter so removed from any understanding of English that the text of *Paradise Lost* would carry less significance for him than any Rorschach blot. But I wonder if even an imagination as brilliantly perverse as Fish's could find an interpreter whose language proved to be that in which the Rorschach blot had been encoded, a language in which the blot could be interpreted as seeking to justify the ways of God to men. One can think of it, but even in thinking it one proves the point that it is supposed to deny. There *is* a difference between a text perceived as encoded in a particular language and one that is perceived as not being in any language at all. In fact, to perceive a text *as* a text is to perceive it as being in a language.

Fish might reply that having a language is part of what he means by being in a community of interpreters. But I would answer by pointing out that no language community is congruous with any interpretive community. Christian exegetes, for example, are not confined to any single language, nor are speakers of any single language compelled to be Christian exegetes. Moreover, a text is bound to its language; it exists as a text only in and through its language. It is not so bound to any interpretive community. Nor are perception and belief as constrained by membership in either a linguistic or an interpretive group as Fish maintains. When Wittgenstein said that our world is bounded by our language he did not say that we had no freedom within the boundaries. If you play chess you can only do certain things with the pieces—or you will no longer be playing chess. But those constraints in themselves never tell you what move to make. Language does not speak—any more than the law of gravity falls. Furthermore, language is changed by speech, though gravity is not changed by any act of falling or flying. But enough analogies—let us look more closely at what Fish does mean by an "interpretive community."

In the introduction to *Is There a Text in This Class?* Fish says that "it is interpretive communities, rather than either the text or the reader, that produce meanings and are responsible for the emergence of formal features" (p. 14). As Fish explains this, we can think and perceive only what our interpretive community allows us to think and perceive. He finds this totalitarian vision completely reassuring. Whatever we think will be right, because we have no choice in the matter. Nor will there be any need to respect the integrity of whatever we are thinking about. The interpretive community will decide for us what is out there and we will duly perceive it. "Not to worry," says Fish. Not to worry? I remember Mr. O'Brien inducting Winston Smith into his interpretive community in *1984.*

Notice what Fish has done. First, he has asserted that readers make texts; then he has shifted his position to say, quite specifically, that meanings are produced by neither text nor reader but by interpretive communities. But he has never made clear what an interpretive community is, how its constituency might be determined, or what could be the source of its awesome power. In practice, he sometimes means simply those who share certain linguistic and cultural information: that is, all those who would understand a certain speech in a certain situation as a request to open the window. At other times he means something like all Christian readers of literary texts. The problem is not just that the size and shape of the "community" change to suit Fish's needs, though that *is* a problem. A greater difficulty is the putting of such things as the English language and Christian typology on the same plane. One may debate whether *Samson*

Agonistes is or is not a Christian poem. But even in order to debate that one must perceive the poem as written in the English language. A Christian reader with no English will not make much of the poem. An English reader with no special Christian interpretive bias can make a good deal of it. The point is that Fish's notion of "community" will not stand examination. He says that "a set of interpretive assumptions is always in force" (p. 284). I would argue that the notion of a single, monolithic *set* of assumptions makes the same totalitarian error that Fish makes in other places. Different, even conflicting, assumptions may preside over any reading of a single text by a single person. It is in fact these very differences—differences *within* the reader, who is never a unified member of a single unified group—it is these very differences that create the space in which the reader exercises a measure of interpretive freedom.

This freedom, however, is most certainly constrained by language. A written text is a set of marks that are as they are only because a certain language was implicated in their composition. A printed text is never only on the page. It is a transaction between what is on the page and the particular linguistic code that originally enabled those marks to carry meaning. This is in fact what distinguishes a written text from a Rorschach blot. Familiarity with a text's linguistic code is assumed by all who discuss the interpretation of literary texts, though some theorists emphasize this and others prefer to ignore it. Fish prefers to ignore it, because any serious consideration of the relationship of both the reader and the writer to language will show that the reader is more constrained than the writer. The reader's choices in "making" meaning are in fact severely limited by the writer's previous choices of what marks to put on the page. But Fish prefers to ignore this set of constraints in order to emphasize the constraints that can be attributed to membership in an interpretive community.

The notion of interpretive communities, he tells us in his introduction, is now "central" to his discourse. It explains everything that was dark before. One thing it explains is the status of the reader: "since the thoughts an individual can think and the mental operations he can perform have their source in some or other interpretive community, he is as much the product of that community (acting as an extension of it) as the meanings it enables him to produce" (p. 14). The reader is simply a product of "some or other" interpretive community, and no one can belong to more than one of these communities at a time. "Members of different communities will disagree," says Fish, and, conversely, those who agree will inevitably be members of the same community. From these premises he draws the truly astonishing conclusion that he has explained "why there are disagreements and why they can be debated in a principled way" (p. 15). This conclusion is astonishing because principled debate is precisely what Fish's theory cannot describe. To agree on the principles that govern critical debate—what counts as evidence and so on—would be to accept membership in the same interpretive community. But members of the same interpretive community, by definition, have no disagreements. Therefore, only those who have no disagreements can settle them in a principled way. The only way out of this Catch-22 (or perhaps we ought to call it Fish-22) is to say that accepting the same principles is not the same as belonging to the same interpretive community. But this only raises in more acute form the question of what an interpretive community might actually be.

If the community makes all selves and governs all interpretations, then any difference in behavior must be due to differences in community. ("Members of different communities will disagree.") It follows from this that there must be as many communities as there are different interpretations. This means that the notion of "interpretive community" in no way coincides with what Thomas Kuhn would call a paradigm or Michel Foucault an episteme. Nor would it coincide with a discipline like literary criticism or even with a school of criticism like Marxist, Freudian, structuralist, feminist, New Critical, speech-act, stylistic, or what-have-you—for the simple reason that so many interpretive disputes occur *within* each of these schools rather than between

them. If an interpretive community is not the same as a critical
school, then what is it and where is it? If every different interpretation is the product of a different community, making different
assumptions and perceiving a different text, how could one
possibly debate or settle such differences? If, as Fish maintains,
there can be no *demonstration* in critical debates (because all
facts are already interpretations), how can there be debates at
all? Fish says that we will have *persuasion* instead of *demonstration*. But I invite him and you to consider just what persuasion
without demonstration would be. If there can be no appeal to
any facts, even by stipulation, then all that is left is self-interest:
the carrot and the stick. How can one have a principled debate
with a person who denies the major premise of debate itself:
namely, that the issues are to be settled by the evidence presented and the conclusions drawn from it rather than by threat-
ening or bribing the judges? You may think I am being unfair.
But Fish honestly admits that his appeal is strictly to self-interest:
"I have been trying to persuade you to believe what I believe
because it is in your own best interests as *you* understand them"
(p. 369).

I, on the other hand, have been trying to demonstrate that
Stanley Fish's notion of "interpretive communities" is a bad idea
because it is full of internal inconsistencies and, finally, misrep-
resents our actual experience as interpreters of texts. I also want
to argue that Fish's whole theory of textual interpretation is both
dangerous and wrong: dangerous because it is partly accurate,
and wrong because it is mistaken about where we are constrained
and where we are free, where we are social and where we are
individual. And it is especially wrong in its notion of what a text
is and what an interpreter does with a text. I will try to show
where Fish goes wrong in these matters by looking at some of the
demonstrations he uses to persuade us to accept his theory.

One of the cleverest demonstrations in *Is There a Text in
This Class?* occurs in the chapter called "How to Recognize a
Poem When You See One." In that chapter Fish tells us that he
was once teaching two different classes that met in the same

room in successive hours. The first class had a linguistic orienta-
tion; the second was doing typological interpretations of seventeenth-century religious poetry. One day he finished the first
class with the following assignment on the board:

Jacobs – Rosenbaum
Levin
Thorne
Hayes
Ohman (?)

When the second class entered the room he told them that this
was a religious poem of the kind they had been studying, and
they duly proceeded to find all sorts of Christian iconography in
the poem, suggesting that "Jacobs – Rosenbaum" was a combination of Jacob's ladder and the rose tree symbolizing the Virgin
Mary, and so on. Fish gives us several pages of clever interpretation, drawing the conclusion that the disposition to see a particular kind of poem in that text led inevitably to the production of
that kind of poem by means of that kind of interpretation.
Beyond that, Fish asserts, "Given a firm belief that they were
confronted by a religious poem, my students would have been
able to turn any list of names into the kind of poem we have
before us now" (p. 328). He then offers an empirical check.
"You can test this assertion by replacing Jacobs – Rosenbaum,
Levin, Thorne, Hayes, and Ohman with names drawn from the
faculty of Kenyon College—Temple, Jordan, Seymour, Daniels,
Star, Church" (p. 328). He doesn't say how the names were
"drawn," but it is clear that this is no random list, and that is no
trivial matter. If you play cards with Stanley Fish, don't let him
bring his own deck.
  My position is simple. I want to argue against Fish's assertion that "any list" can be interpreted as a Christian poem in the
seventeenth-century manner. I also want to attack the larger
assertion that the text offers no resistance or encouragement to
particular interpretive strategies. This assertion is made by Fish
throughout his book, sometimes in his various recantations of

earlier positions. For instance, in his brilliant analysis of Shakespeare's *Coriolanus* from the perspective of speech-act theory, he claims that the analysis works well because *Coriolanus* is a play about speech acts. In the recantation he says that this is not so: "If any reader is persuaded by the analysis it will not be because it accords with the facts of the play but because he will have first been persuaded to the interpretive assumptions in the light of which the facts as I cite them seem inescapable" (p. 200).

Perhaps the most striking thing about this recantation is its faith in the power of assumptions to make a particular view of facts inescapable, or rather to constitute a particular set of facts. This is based upon a mistaken interpretation of Thomas Kuhn's paradigm theory, which is often abused by humanists for their own ends. In Kuhn's view, scientists working within a certain paradigm keep turning up anomalous facts, which ultimately lead to a crisis in the paradigm itself. But in Fish's view there can be no anomalous facts, since all facts are constructed by the assumptions of an interpretive community and texts offer no resistance to acts of interpretation. This is why Fish's class can perceive a religious poem in any text that their teacher tells them is a religious poem. They are in an interpretive community and Stanley Fish is the king of that community.

But suppose that what had been left on the blackboard was not simply a list of names in a vaguely emblematic shape. Suppose the text had taken the form a prose statement of the assignment that read as follows:

> For next Thursday read the essays in the
> Jacobs and Rosenbaum anthology by Levin,
> Thorne, Hayes, and Ohmann.

If this were the case, would Fish have told the second class that the text constituted a religious poem? If he had, would they have succeeded so splendidly in perceiving it as one? I think the answer to both questions is, "No." To any competent reader of English the prosaic quality of this sentence would make it difficult to perceive it as poetry. I am not saying it couldn't be done.

I'm saying it wouldn't be done. And if it were done it would require prodigies of double-think. The reader would be *aware* of the labor of making this poem out of something else, and so would perceive it as already being that something else. In other words, a gap between the given text and the constructed poem would open up. To say this is not to insist that poetry and prose are absolute categories. They are culture-bound, of course, and subject to change. But members of a culture that has such categories will be able to assign some texts to one category and some to the other, by looking at the properties of the texts through the grid of the categories.

Fish is so anxious to insist that culture shapes perception that he denies to objects any real existence even *within* a cultural context. His mechanism for accomplishing this is to assert that all perceived differences are the result of different mechanisms of perception. It is like saying that bluejays and robins can never be seen by the same person because any person will be either in the bluejay community or the robin community and therefore will see only one or the other. This may sound ludicrous, but it is exactly what Fish is saying when he argues that "*Coriolanus* is a speech-act play for me because it is with speech-act theory in mind that I approached the play" (p. 200). I would say, on the other hand, that one ought to be able to approach a play with speech-act theory in mind only to discover that it is not really a very suitable approach for that play, or, conversely, one might say that speech-act theory is especially relevant to plays as opposed, say, to meditative discourse, because plays, by definition, enact speech. But formulations such as these are denied by Fish because they imply both some reality in the texts and some freedom in the interpreter—neither of which Fish wants to admit. We can see this clearly if we return to his typology classroom.

As a check on Fish's thesis I have tried to show that a change in the text that leaves all its original words present but embeds them in a prose syntax would affect the ability of a group to perceive it as a poem. Now, suppose we do it the other way,

keeping the structure as Fish displayed it but offering another
list of names, not "drawn" by Fish for this purpose but listed by
him (in this order) later in the same chapter.

Abrams—Hirsch
Reichert
Graff
Holland
Bleich (?)

Your determined Christian typologist might get his teeth into
Abrams by bringing out the latent Abraham, but after that it
would be tough going, because the names carry almost no semantic weight in English. Fish might do better by shifting to
German, but a shift to German would demonstrate that the
relationship between a text and its language is real and prior
to all interpretive gestures, something that Fish regularly ignores or denies. The Christian exegete with no German will be
forced to admit a difference between this text and the Jacobs—
Rosenbaum text. Furthermore, I would argue that even the text
proposed by Fish (the Jacobs—Rosenbaum text) would not be
mistaken by a competent exegete for a poem by Herbert or
Donne. It is a list only, lacking in the predicative syntax that such
poems regularly have. It might be seen as notes for a poem or
fragments of a poem but not as a whole poem. If the poem
appears to have a syntax, it is because of the question mark,
present only because of Fish's uncertainty about the spelling of
Ohmann's name, which he has in fact got wrong. The correct
spelling, however, would not yield (in English) the reading "Oh
man," which is a crucial element in the Christian reading of the
Jacobs—Rosenbaum text. Fish has also provided us with what
must be the unique appearance of the word "Rosenbaum" in
English metaphysical poetry. Can one really believe that students mistook this Fishy text for a poem by even the most
minuscule metaphysical poet? Heterogeneous ideas yoked together by violence? Where's the yoke? The yoke, I believe, is on
anyone who accepts this anecdote as true. Surely Fish's students

were playing a game either with or on their teacher. Texts have a
certain reality. A change in a letter or a mark of punctuation can
force us to perceive them differently, read them differently, and
interpret them differently.

Almost all of Fish's demonstrations are striking, clever, and
witty, but they seldom demonstrate what he says they do. Take
the case of Pat Kelly's two home runs in one baseball game. Fish
notes that Kelly, an outfielder for the Baltimore Orioles, is a
born-again Christian, who attributes his achievements on the
field to divine intervention in human affairs. Fish contrasts Kelly
with Michael Janofsky, a sports writer who complains that one
cannot talk to Kelly "on a strictly baseball level. He does not
view his home runs as merely a part of athletic competition.
They are part of his religious experience" (Janofsky, quoted by
Fish, p. 270). Fish uses this as a demonstration of his theory of
interpretation. For Janofsky, Fish argues, the "strictly baseball
level" is the literal meaning, and the Christian view is an interpretation that has replaced the literal meaning; but, for Kelly,
Fish insists, the Christian view is now the literal or natural one,
having replaced the baseball view for Kelly when he joined the
Christian interpretive community.

This example illustrates perfectly the major problem in
Fish's theory: his refusal to see any difference between the
primary system in which a text is encoded and secondary systems
that can only be brought to bear by an interpreter who compre-
hends the primary system. In the case of Kelly and Janofsky, the
primary system is baseball itself. Kelly's deed constitutes the
text: driving the ball out of the park twice, making a circuit of
the bases each time. It is the language or code of baseball that
enables us to interpret this as "hitting two home runs in one
game." Without the code of baseball—the rules of the game—
this interpretation could not be made. Hitting two balls into the
seats during batting practice would not be interpreted as hitting
two home runs in one game, even if the hitter decided to run
around the bases after each one of them, which he normally
would not do. I doubt if Kelly himself would find a batting

practice blast significant enough to have required divine intervention. Kelly may need batting practice, but God, we trust,
does not.

Without the primary system or code of baseball, Kelly's
deeds would be meaningless, a kind of noise, if in fact they could
be performed at all. The deed and the system, the text and the
code, are united. Without a code (or codes) no text can be either
written or interpreted, and the codes that enable a text to carry
meanings cannot be discarded without losing those meanings.
Seeing the power of God—or the power of Wheaties, for that
matter—in Kelly's home runs depends upon all concerned perceiving them as home runs in the first place. If a ballplayer says,
"I didn't hit them home runs, God did," this would be construed
by all competent interpreters as dependent upon the prior understanding that (a) two home runs had been hit, and (b) that
they had been attributed to the speaker.

I am suggesting that the notion of a single interpretive
community presiding over every act of interpretation is mistaken
and misleading. Kelly does not give up the baseball interpretation of his deeds, he grafts another interpretation onto the
baseball interpretation. Most acts that justify the term "interpretation" at all involve the use of several codes, and most
interpretive disputes can be usefully seen as disputes over the
proper hierarchy of codes: whether a particular code is relevant
at all, whether one code is more or less relevant than another,
and so on. Where Fish sees interpretive communities remotely
controlling acts of interpretation by individuals suffering from
the illusion of freedom, I see individuals with many codes, some
more and some less relevant, trying to see which ones will serve
best in dealing with structures that have their own necessities.
From my point of view the notion of interpretive community
suggests a process that is too monolithic to represent adequately
the agonies of choice that confront actual interpreters, who
often have at their disposal more codes than they can use.

Codes, of course, constrain. It is only the multiplicity of
codes that allows humans scope for any freedom or choice in

writing or reading. There are, for instance, codes that belong primarily to language and others that are features of the pragmatic interchanges of speech. One can, for example, repeat a verbal formula in such a way that posture or intonation will weaken or subvert the words. In the spaces provided by such conflicts of coding we find much of our freedom and our verbal art. The codes governing verbal interchange have come under serious investigation in recent years by the speech-act philosophers, who have developed notions like the "cooperative principle" of H. P. Grice as ways of describing nonverbal constraints on speech and its interpretation. Fish has moved into this area, too, avoiding Grice but attacking John Searle's description of direct and indirect speech acts, which is very similar to Grice's distinction between saying and implying. Searle distinguishes between two uses of the same verbal expression: "I have to study for an exam." In one case it is simply a statement about the speaker, and in the other, when made in reply to "Let's go to the movies," it also means something like, "No. I refuse to go to the movies with you," thus carrying a secondary or indirect meaning. Fish says no to this, insisting that in the second case there is only one meaning, the rejection of the proposal, and that it is primary.

This objection to Searle is similar to many objections Fish has made to critics who accept a distinction between primary and secondary or literal and figurative meanings. For Fish all meanings are equally literal because no meaning is ever literal. All meanings are situational and contextual. We should note that this view implies that being in a speech-act situation is the same thing as being in an interpretive community. But in practice Fish presents the idea of interpretive communities as relatively stable entities, presiding over interpretation from afar, while situations are volatile and personal, strictly ad hoc. One is always in a situation, he insists, and one is always in a community. They are different, but they both totally constrain interpretation. Much of this confusion stems from Fish's having constructed his notion of interpretive communities from two conflicting sources. One source is David Bleich's notion of "interpretive communities," by which Bleich means a place like a classroom or a psychoanalytic session in which human beings intersubjectively negotiate interpretations, striving for a consensus. The other principal source is Thomas Kuhn's notion of "paradigms," a set of assumptions and procedures that links all researchers in a given discipline at a particular time. Connecting these two not exactly compatible views in Fish's scheme is the ultra-semiotic or post-structuralist assumption that sign-systems affect perception but that the world does not, and that such sign-systems are structures of pure difference, untrammeled by outside influence. It is a tribute to Fish's consummate rhetoric that he can make this festering mass of contradictions and ungrounded assumptions disappear under the apparently single term, "interpretive community."

But to return to the critique of Searle: Fish insists that if the statement "I have to study for an exam" is made in response to a proposal to attend a movie and is therefore interpreted as a rejection—a rejection is all it is. It is most emphatically not a statement about the speaker's plans *plus* a rejection of the proposal; it is a rejection only, because the situation totally controls what it can mean. "A sentence . . . always has the meaning that has been conferred on it by the situation in which it is uttered" (p. 291). All of this seems to me highly dubious, and it should be easy to show that this is so. We have only to imagine the originator of the movie proposal going on to see the film and meeting a friend of the rejector who asks where old so-and-so is. Will the proposer reply, "I don't know; I asked him to come to the movies but all he said was no." Of course he will not say that. He will say that old so-and-so is studying for an exam. How does he know? He knows because old so-and-so told him and used that message to carry the secondary meaning of rejection of the proposal. In other words, when Fish says that only one meaning is present, he is wrong.

We might observe also that such solicitude for the situation of utterance need not apply to oral speech acts only; it could be applied to written texts as well. A written text is the record of a transaction between a writer and the language in which the text is composed. It is indeed always the product of a situation. Should it not, then, to quote Fish (p. 291), "have the meaning that has been conferred on it by the situation in which it is uttered"? If this principle were applied to written texts, then all interpreters of literature would have to take as their primary goal the recovery of the codes (linguistic, generic, ideological) that constituted the situations of the texts they have chosen to interpret. And I would argue that in actual practice virtually all competent interpreters—and I most emphatically include Stanley Fish, Roland Barthes, and Jacques Derrida in this category—have attended to these primary matters, whether they admit it or not. Who cares about the text? We all do.

We care about texts for many reasons, not the least of which is that they bring us news that alters our way of interpreting things. If this were not the case, the Gospels and the teachings of Karl Marx would have fallen upon deaf ears. Textual power is ultimately power to change the world.

DETEXT

Il n'y a pas de hors-texte.

Jacques Derrida,
Of Grammatology

But in the first week Watt's words had
not yet begun to fail him, or Watt's world
to become unspeakable.

Samuel Beckett,
Watt

Nothing outside the text for Derrida; nothing inside it for Beckett. Between the unspeakable world and the text that will never shut up, where are we? Text may never end, but every book is bound to be finished. We achieve finitude by certain choices that are both textual and worldly. If we choose to be English teachers in America, for instance, we have the same reality within that textual world as any characters do in the books wherein they are inscribed. Because a cagey teacher is a caged teacher, we cannot adopt certain theoretical positions that we can and should entertain. My enterprise in this book has been to take the teaching situation as a theoretical position from which to look at other theories that impinge upon the study and teaching of texts. Large sections of my own text were written first to clarify things for myself, my students, and my colleagues. I hope the final and all too finite versions bound between these covers may perform the same function for others.

NOTES

PRETEXT

Epigraph: Umberto Eco, *The Name of the Rose*, trans. William Weaver (New York: Warner Books, 1984), p. 68.

CHAPTER 1

Epigraphs: Bertolt Brecht, *Brecht on Theatre*, trans. John Willett (New York: Hill & Wang, 1964), p. 34.
Michel Foucault, *The Archaeology of Knowledge*, trans. A. M. Sheridan-Smith (New York: Irvington Publishers, 1972), p. 51.
1 Clifford Geertz, *The Interpretation of Cultures* (New York: Basic Books, 1973).
2 Paula Johnson, "Writing Programs and the English Department," *Profession '80*, p. 15.
3 Erving Goffman, *Frame Analysis: An Essay on the Organization of Experience* (New York: Harper and Row, 1974).
4 Frank Kermode, *The Genesis of Secrecy: On the Interpretation of Narrative* (Cambridge, MA: Harvard University Press, 1979).
5 Paul Ricoeur, *Freud and Philosophy: An Essay on Interpretation*, trans. Denis Savage (New Haven: Yale University Press, 1970); Fredric Jameson, *The Political Unconscious: Narrative as a Socially Symbolic Act* (Ithaca: Cornell University Press, 1981).

CHAPTER 2

Epigraph: Umberto Eco, *The Role of the Reader: Explorations in the Semiotics of Texts* (Bloomington: Indiana University Press, 1979), p. 214.

1 Quotations are from a 1930 printing of Ernest Hemingway, *In Our Time* (New York: Charles Scribner's Sons).

2 Robert Scholes, *Semiotics and Interpretation* (New Haven: Yale University Press, 1982).

CHAPTER 3

Epigraph: Eco, *The Role of the Reader*, p. 39.

1 George Lukács, *History and Class Consciousness: Studies in Marxist Dialectics*, trans. Rodney Livingstone (Cambridge, MA: MIT Press, 1971).

2 Walter L. Adamson, *Hegemony and Revolution: A Study of Antonio Gramsci's Political and Cultural Theory* (Berkeley: University of California Press, 1980), p. 81.

3 Kenneth G. Johnston, "Hemingway and Mantegna: The Bitter Nail Holes," *Journal of Narrative Technique* (1971), cited in Jackson J. Benson, *The Short Stories of Ernest Hemingway* (Durham: Duke University Press, 1975).

4 Quotations are from Ernest Hemingway, *A Farewell to Arms* (New York: Charles Scribner's Sons, a 1932 printing), and *For Whom the Bell Tolls* (New York: Charles Scribner's Sons, 1940).

CHAPTER 4

Epigraph: Eco, *The Role of the Reader*, p. 22.

1 Ernest Hemingway, *Death in the Afternoon* (New York: Charles Scribner's Sons, 1932).

CHAPTER 5

Epigraph: Edward Said, *The World, the Text, and the Critic* (Cambridge, MA: Harvard University Press, 1983), pp. 3–4.

1 Terry Eagleton, *Literary Theory: An Introduction* (Minneapolis: University of Minnesota Press, 1983).

2 John Berger, *Ways of Seeing* (Penguin Books, 1977).

3 Paul de Man, *Allegories of Reading: Figural Language in Rousseau, Nietzsche, Rilke, and Proust* (New Haven: Yale University Press, 1979).

4 Michel Foucault, *Discipline and Punish: The Birth of the Prison*, trans. Alan Sheridan (New York: Pantheon, 1978).

CHAPTER 6

Epigraph: Bertrand Russell, *My Philosophical Development* (Unwin Paperback Series, 1975), p. 110.

1 Jonathan Culler, *On Deconstruction: Theory and Criticism after Structuralism* (Ithaca: Cornell University Press, 1982); *Ferdinand de Saussure* (Penguin Books, 1977).

2 Ferdinand de Saussure, *Course in General Linguistics*, trans. Wade Baskin (New York: McGraw-Hill, 1966).

3 Jonathan Culler, *Structuralist Poetics: Structuralism, Linguistics, and the Study of Literature* (Ithaca: Cornell University Press, 1975); *The Pursuit of Signs: Semiotics, Literature, Deconstruction* (Ithaca: Cornell University Press, 1981).

4 Ferruccio Rossi-Landi, *Ideologies of Linguistic Relativity* (The Hague: Mouton, 1973), p. 56.

5 See Hans Arsleff's important collection of essays, *From Locke to Saussure* (Minneapolis: University of Minnesota Press, 1982).

6 John Locke, *An Essay Concerning Human Understanding* (Dover edition), 2:8.

7 Jacques Derrida, *Positions*, trans. Alan Bass (Chicago: University of Chicago Press, 1981).

8 Charles Peirce, *Collected Papers*, ed. Charles Hartshorne and Paul Weiss (Cambridge, MA: Harvard University Press, 1974), 5:332, ¶ 5.484.

9 Jacques Derrida, "Structure, Sign, and Play in the Discourse of the Human Sciences," in Richard Macksey and Eugenio Donato, eds., *The Structuralist Controversy: The Languages of Criticism and the Sciences of Man* (Baltimore: Johns Hopkins University Press, 1972).

10 Jacques Derrida, *Speech and Phenomena: And Other Essays on Husserl's Theory of Signs*, trans. David B. Allison (Evanston: Northwestern University Press, 1973).

11 W. V. O. Quine, *Ontological Relativity and Other Essays* (New York: Columbia University Press, 1969).

12 Jacques Derrida, *Dissemination*, trans. Barbara Johnson (Chicago: University of Chicago Press, 1981).

13 Quoted from the 1916 edition of Aphra Behn's *Works*, volume 5 (reissued by Benjamin Blom in 1967), p. 182.

14 Lennard J. Davis, *Factual Fictions: The Origins of the English Novel* (New York: Columbia University Press, 1983), pp. 109, 110.

15 David Hume, *Enquiries Concerning Human Understanding*, Section 19.

16 Ludwig Wittgenstein, *Remarks on Colour*, ed. G. E. Anscombe, trans. L. L. McAlister and M. Schattle (Berkeley: University of California Press, 1978).

17 W. V. O. Quine, *Word and Object* (Cambridge, MA: MIT Press, 1960).

18 David Lindsay, *A Voyage to Arcturus* (New York: Ballantine Books, 1973; originally published in 1920), p. 53.

CHAPTER 7

Epigraphs: Jacques Derrida, *Edmund Husserl's "The Origin of Geometry": An Introduction*, trans. John P. Leavey (York Beach, ME: Nicolas-Hays, 1977), p. 137. Ursula K. Le Guin, "It Was a Dark and Stormy Night," in W. J. T. Mitchell, ed., *On Narrative* (Chicago: University of Chicago Press, 1981), p. 195.

1 Ian MacLean, *The Renaissance Notion of Woman* (Cambridge: Cambridge University Press, 1980), pp. 2–3.

2 Ursula K. Le Guin, *The Left Hand of Darkness* (New York: Walker and Co., 1969).

3 Ursula K. Le Guin, *The Wind's Twelve Quarters* (New York: Harper and Row, 1975).

4 Jacques Derrida, *Of Grammatology*, trans. Gayatri Chakravorty Spivak (Baltimore: Johns Hopkins University Press, 1977).

CHAPTER 8

Epigraph: Herman Melville, *Moby-Dick* (New York: W. W. Norton, 1967), p. 277.

1 Ezra Pound, *ABC of Reading* (Norfolk, CT: New Directions, n.d.); John Steinbeck and Edward F. Ricketts, *Sea of Cortez: A Leisurely Journal of Travel and Research* (Mamaroneck: Paul P. Appel, 1971).

2 Michel Foucault, *The Archaeology of Knowledge*, trans. A. M. Sheridan-Smith (New York: Irvington Publishers, 1972).

3 Lane Cooper, *Louis Agassiz as a Teacher: Illustrative Extracts on His Method of Instruction* (Ithaca: The Comstock Publishing Co., 1917).

4 Northrop Frye, *Anatomy of Criticism* (Princeton: Princeton University Press, 1957).

5 Edward Lurie, *Louis Agassiz, A Life in Science* (Chicago: University of Chicago Press, 1960).

6 Thomas Kuhn, *The Structure of Scientific Revolutions* (Chicago: University of Chicago Press, 1970).

CHAPTER 9

Epigraph: P. D. James, *The Skull Beneath the Skin* (New York: Warner Books, 1983), p. 140.

1 Stanley Fish, *Is There a Text in This Class?* (Cambridge, MA: Harvard University Press, 1980).

DETEXT

Epigraphs: Jacques Derrida, *Of Grammatology*, p. 158; Samuel Beckett, *Watt* (New York: Grove Press, 1959), p. 85.

INDEX

173

Intentional fallacy, 47
Interpretant, 90, 109
Interpretation, 5, 53; and criticism,
14, 15, 23; and reading, 22;
pedagogy of, 30; and semantic and
syntactic fields, 48
Interpretive communities, 150–64
passim
Intertextuality, 31, 136, 147

James, Henry, 24, 59
James, P. D., *The Skull Beneath the
Skin*, 149
Jameson, Fredric, 31, 49, 74, 75, 91;
The Political Unconscious, 14, 16,
80, 84; and interpretation, 48
Johnson, Barbara, 99
Johnson, Paula, "Writing Programs
and the English Department," 5
Johnston, Kenneth, "Hemingway and
Mantegna: The Bitter Nail
Holes," 45

Kermode, Frank, *The Genesis of
Secrecy*, 11
Kilmer, Joyce, 62, 136
Kuhn, Thomas S., 4, 143, 164; *The
Structure of Scientific Revolutions*,
143

Leavis, F. R., 35
Le Guin, Ursula: "It Was a Dark and
Stormy Night," 111; *The Left
Hand of Darkness*, 115–28
passim; *The Wind's Twelve
Quarters*, 116; "Winter's King,"
116
Lindsay, David, *A Voyage to
Arcturus*, 108
Linguistic difference (differentiation),
106, 122
Literariness, 74
Literature, and scripture, 12–15
Locke, John, 8, 89, 90, 93; *An Essay
Concerning Human Under-
standing*, 89
Lukács, George, 38, 43, 54; *Writer
and Critic*, 38; *History and Class
Consciousness*, 43
Lurie, Edward, *Louis Agassiz, A Life
in Science*, 142, 143

Macksey and Donato, *The
Structuralist Controversy*, 92
MacLean, Ian, *The Renaissance
Notion of Woman*, 115, 125
Mantegna, Andrea, 44, 45, 51
Marx (Marxism), 16, 80, 81, 165
Mediation, 81–82
Melville, Herman, *Moby-Dick*, 129
Metaphysical poetry, 160
Milton, John, 14, 152–54 passim;
Paradise Lost, 152; *Samson
Agonistes*, 153–54
Modernism, 23, 24, 38, 71
More, Thomas, 116, 120
Moses, 15
Mussolini, Benito, 43, 53

Narrative coding, 21–22
Naturalism, 35, 37, 38, 45, 54; as
cultural code, 35; in Hemingway,
37–38, 54
New Criticism (New Critics), 18, 21,
24, 31, 47, 52, 79, 137; and
classroom practice, 18, 31; and
modernism, 24; and intention, 47;
and Paul de Man, 79
Nietzsche, Friedrich, "On Truth and
Lies," 141
Nominalization, 97
Non-literature, 5, 6, 7, 8

Objective correlative, 71
Ogden and Richards, 91, 92
Otherness (the Other), 50, 59, 124,
125

Paradigmatic, 103
Peirce, Charles S., 31, 91, 92, 99; and
unlimited semiosis, 90; and
Jonathan Culler, 102
Pentateuch, 15
Platonism, 136
Point of view, 28, 56, 61
Pope, Alexander: "Windsor Forest,"
145, 146; *Dunciad*, 146–47;
"Essay on Criticism," 147
Post-Structuralism, 2, 80, 86, 103,
105, 164; and reference, 80, 86;
and view of language, 105; and
perception, 164. *See also* Derrida,
Deconstruction